To Daph
A

barcode: D1111698

'on

PRIME
ANGUS

With Yatitude,

Angus

ANGUS LIND

Arthur Hardy Enterprises INC

Published by
Arthur Hardy Enterprises, Inc.
230 Devon Drive
Mandeville, LA 70448

ISBN 0-930892-26-7

Special thanks to:
Liuzza's Restaurant & Bar on Bienville Street
Mary Lou Atkinson
Jerry McLeod

Art Director: David Johnson
Typography: Kristina Ericksen
Cover Photo: Syndey Byrd

The columns in this book were originally published in *The Times-Picayune.*

DEDICATION

For Anne,
my best friend, wife & love of my life

For my beloved family:
Patrick, Katie & Tim,
who keep me young at heart

For my mentor,
Billy Rainey,
the best damn newspaperman
I ever knew

For Coaches
Tony Reginelli & Skeets Tuohy,
who kept me laughing
through the tough times

Introduction

Retiring from *The Times-Picayune* was one of the most difficult decisions of my life. A great many people don't love their jobs. I did. And I loved the people I worked with. Still do.

I began at the end of a golden era, and was lucky and blessed to have been a part of it – at *The States-Item*, the old sensationalistic afternoon newspaper, where the newsroom was wild and crazy and loud and smoky. The hard-working, hard-drinking old-timers were the guys who taught me how to be a newspaperman. We worked hard, getting in at the crack of dawn, made three different deadlines and then . . . we partied. We all seemed to have the attitude that in New Orleans, if you die of old age, it's your fault.

I still tell people it's hard to believe I got paid for having so much damn fun.

The 39 years went fast. Retirement? I never once thought about retirement.

But after weeks of soul-searching, I knew it was the right decision. Time to move on. Time to spend more time with my wife and family, time to smell the roses, walk the shoreline and listen to the sound of the ocean, play more golf, bet on more horses, travel, and forget about writing for a while.

So what happened? Why this book? I had no plans for a book, certainly not this quickly. Was I having trouble dealing with no deadlines to meet after four decades of meeting them? Did I miss writing? Was I going to be one of those guys who flunks retirement?

No, it was none of those. It was you, the readers.

My last column appeared in The Times-Picayune on May 31, 2009. Not long after that, the phone started ringing and the emails started coming. They didn't stop for a long time. I was humbled and overwhelmed – and stunned — not only by the nice comments readers made, but the numbers of them – there were hundreds and hundreds.

Many of them suggested I should do a book of columns. And when I started getting out and about in the late afternoon, as I am prone to do, I got more and more inquiries about putting together a collection of columns.

Weeks went by. The book suggestions persisted. I still wasn't convinced. So I had a conversation with Susan Larson, *The Times-Picayune* book editor, lovingly known as the "Book Mama" because of her passion for her job. She said one thing to me: "Do it. You've got to do it." Her endorsement and encouragement meant everything.

So . . . I found a willing publisher and kindred spirit, Arthur Hardy, the Mardi Gras historian, television Carnival commentator and publisher of his own *Mardi Gras Guide* for decades, and many books. We quickly hit it off. He is as N'Awlins as I am. And then there was the cooperation of my longtime employer, *The Times-Picayune*, Publisher Ashton Phelps Jr., Editor Jim Amoss and Managing Editor Dan Shea — without which this book would never have come to fruition. I thank them.

Along the way, there have been plenty of people who need thanking: Retired *States-Item* Editor Walter Cowan, who hired me, Copy Desk Editor Tom Gregory and the best re-write man anywhere, Billy Earl Rainey – the biggest influence on my career. And three outstanding editors of the Living section through the years: Bettye Anding, James O'Byrne and Mark Lorando. They all put up with my shenanigans, caught my errors and made me a better writer. Editors don't get enough thanks.

Going through thousands of columns and stories and boiling it down to sixty-something is no simple task. But it was fun turning back the clock, and it could not have been done without the wonderful cooperation and research of my pal Danny Gamble and the T-P library staff.

So here we are. There are many different subject matters inside, and that's what a collection is all about – it's a sampling of New Orleans. Among others, you'll find columns about some quintessential New Orleans characters, many of whom are no longer in our midst – but need to be remembered because they are/were the very fabric that makes up this city's unconventional, unpredictable, quirky story.

You'll also find dialects and dialogues that are memorable more because of who said it and when it was said than its importance – and also because in many cases it is hopefully amusing.

I hope the book captures how much I love this city, and I hope you enjoy it.

— A.L.

Table Of Contents

CHAPTER 1
Life in the Crazy Crescent

What's a Yat? If Ya Gotta Ask, Ya Mudda's an Erster

April 18, 1977 in The States-Item, the very first column

Here's one for you tavern crawlers to argue about: Where did "Where ya at?" come from.

It's not the burning issue of our times, compared to the price of crawfish or shrimp, but neither is it a meaningless inquiry. "Where ya at?" or "Where y'at?" has become a traditional New Orleans greeting, almost a way of life, a state of mind. It is easily as worthy of debate as the last Dodger Don Larsen retired when he pitched his perfect game for the Yankees in the '56 Series.

Some say the phrase is a cultural stamp – immediately placing the speaker at the corner of Fourth and Chippewa, wearing a sleeveless undershirt and drinking a Dixie Beer. But I don't buy that. A lot of those people who stood at Fourth and Chippewa, wore sleeveless undershirts and drank Dixie Beer have moved to Jefferson Parish, where they stand around their lawns in sleeveless undershirts and drink Dixie Beer.

Seventy-five percent of the people in the greater New Orleans area say, "Where ya at?" It cuts across social classes, color lines and parish boundaries.

Was it the Irish Channel's Crowbar gang who coined the phrase back in the 19th century? Was it some guy around the corner from where Hap Glaudi grew up in the Ninth Ward? Or was it, as one guy suggested to me, Hap himself?

The whole subject came up the other night when an out-of-town friend asked me about a word he had heard.

"What is a yat?" he asked.

"A Yat," I told him, capitalizing the "Y" in my mind, "is a person who says, 'Where ya at?' "

"Why does he say that?"

"Oh, just being friendly, instead of hello, how's it going?

"That's all he does and they call him a Yat?"

"No, there's more to it than that. It's kind of an ethnic thing. See, there were these areas of the city where people spoke kind of a Brooklynese. You know, dis and dat, the cab driver accent. The guy who asks, 'Where ya goin', Joisey?' or the newspaper hawker who yells, 'Another moiduh! Read all about it!'

"I guess you heard it most in the Irish Channel and Ninth Ward, but now you can find it all over."

What I really wanted to tell him about was a guy I saw at a Jazz-Lakers game the night the Jazz set the NBA attendance record. Kareem Abdul-Jabbar had just been called for a foul and was arguing with the ref over the call. A guy three seats away from me stood up ready for the kill.

He was wearing dark pants hiked up to about mid-chest, had white socks on, and the top button of his double-knit shirt was buttoned. He was chewing gum, had a beer in his hand and another on the floor, and blood vessels on the side of his head were bursting.

"Jabbaw, ya mudda's an erster!" he shouted.

I will never forget that, whatever it meant, as long as I live. That, I thought to myself, is a thoroughbred Yat, Constance and Foist bloodlines. No cross-breeding there, not a trace of Chalmette Yat in him. But I was afraid I would be getting ahead of myself if I told my friend about the guy too soon.

And before I get accused of being a college punk who only wears button-down collars and grew up in the 14th Ward (which is true), let me tell you two things: First, I have a lot of friends who are Yats I wouldn't swap for all the blue blood on State Street. And second, I am constantly guilty of two of the most critical Yat criteria:

I always say, "Where ya at?" And I always "go by" Graffagnino's or Bruno's for a beer. A Yat doesn't "go to" or "stop at" Acy's for a

9

beer, he "goes by" Acy's. If a guy asks you to stop at Acy's for a beer, forget it – you can book it that the guy doesn't have a trace of Yat in him.

"Have you ever heard the story about what the Brooklyn cab drivers said when they found out pitcher Waite Hoyt had injured himself right before a big series?" I asked my friend.

"No," he said.

"They said Hurt is hoyt."

"What I'm trying to tell you is that these people, the Yats, they butcher Webster like you wouldn't believe. They make mincemeat of vowels and consonants. They live with their mudda and fadda, they look for Foist and Thoid streets, they go by their gramma's house, they woik hard, spend Sundays in choich and drink plenty of beer wid ersters."

"Ersters?"

"Oysters. In fact, one night when Bob Maestri was mayor, he was eating at Antoine's with FDR, and after Oysters Rockefeller had been served, Maestri was sort of at a loss for words. He turned to FDR and said, 'Mr. President, how'd ya like dem ersters?'"

Yats also "axe" questions, put dishers in "da zink," "ogle da goils," "flush da terlet," and "put erl in da caw." When they get excited, they say, "Jesus Gawd!" And if you say Mel-POM-e-nee to a Yat, he's liable to hit you – the street is pronounced Mel-po-MEAN."

Dr. George Reinecke, professor of English at the University of New Orleans, has studied speech patterns in different areas of the city, including the Ninth Ward and the Irish Channel.

He has concluded that the confusion of the "ir" and "oi" sound, as in girl and goil, resulted in an over-correction by the speaker. Because they pronounced girl and first, goil and foist, they made toilets terlets and tin foil tin ferl.

Reinecke's favorite expression is "Wrap da toikey in tin ferl and baste it wid olive erl."

He suspects that the Irish immigrant is the original reason for the confusion of oi and ir sounds, and wherever the Irish Channel, or Yat, dialect originated, it is probably common to three-quarters of the whites in the New Orleans area who are native born.

But the origin of "Where ya at?" is tougher, he says. "The origins of slang are practically impossible to find. I learned the phrase in the 1940s, used by both blacks and whites. And it seems to be particular to New Orleans. I don't have any strong evidence of it being used elsewhere.

"All it takes is a couple of smart guys drinking a beer on a corner to think up a new phrase and it catches on. And where do you find them?"

Which takes us back to Fourth and Chippewa.

Paul Revere in Drag

June 25, 2000

In a doorway on Decatur Street, right past a Samuel Adams beer truck with a parking ticket on it, sat Paul Revere in drag, ponytail and triangular patriot hat paired with a mini-skirt. His red eyes and flushed face were staring toward a small park in the middle of the intersection where there is a statue most people know to be Joan of Arc.

Where else but the French Quarter could you find the leader of the Boston Tea Party (Adams) immortalized on a beer truck, the silversmith who rode to Concord warning Americans the British were coming (Revere) wearing a skirt and the canonized Maid of Orleans looking as if Goldfinger had done his thing – and all in one block?

At Paul Revere's side was what was left of a half gallon of Jack Daniel's black. Someone asked what he was staring at.

"Some guy on a horse, like one of them knights in armor," he replied.

"That's not a knight – that's Joan of Arc," said a nearby streets worker.

"Oh yeah, the woman who burned all those people at the stake," said Paul Revere.

Exactly. Joan of Arc — the woman who burned all those people at the stake. Fractured history – that's what can happen when you cross too much of Lynchburg, Tennessee's finest product with the Salem Witch Trials, an equestrian statue and a mind that may not have a total grasp of 15th century Europe and one of its legends.

The French Quarter is a never-ending source of amusement, if not a font of historical accuracy. Every time I go there, I feel as though I had been airlifted into a European city thousands of miles away. It's a total getaway. It's a place to hang out that is unmatched. I can get down there and forget about everything.

It's the greatest people-watching venue anywhere, and I never get tired of playing tourist – listening to the street musicians, looking at the ironwork (or sunbathers) on balconies, the old bricks, the courtyards and the cathedral – even some lost soul who thinks he's Paul Revere.

Speaking of the cathedral, I took my post near the cannon at Washington Park on the Moonwalk, the best vantage point for tourist watching and eavesdropping. Group after group walked up, gawked and then took the Kodak Moment classic picture of Jackson Square with St. Louis Cathedral in the background.

"You know, Harry, it kind of reminds me of the Magic Kingdom at Disney World, don'tcha think?" a woman told her husband, who answered with an inconclusive grunt.

Well, I guess you could also make a case that the Taj Mahal looks like Harrah's Casino and Gallier Hall looks like the Parthenon – especially if you had logged some quality time in the elixir emporiums the Vieux Carre is most noted for.

In fairness, though, I've never seen a Lucky Dog vendor in front of the Magic Kingdom – there's the obvious difference. Otherwise, they would be identical.

At Jackson Square, a buggy driver was telling his latest victims that the statue of Andrew Jackson looks nothing like Old Hickory, that the general never tipped his hat to anyone, as he is doing on horseback in this equestrian statue. Possibly this has some merit to it. Maybe somebody kept track of hat tippers back then.

But more importantly, if you were riding a horse and he reared up on his back legs, you'd probably be trying to get him under control instead of taking your lid off and saluting someone. Just a guess. Unless you were part of the Lipizzaner troupe which comes to town every once in a while.

I also learned quite a bit about the Baroness Pontalba, the woman responsible for building the two famous row houses on either side of Jackson Square. First, she was ugly as sin and second, maybe the ugliest woman to ever show her face in America.

A quick review: The Baroness Pontalba:

Was a Julia Roberts clone.

Was a dead ringer for Cameron Diaz.

Had a face made for radio.

She had to be ugly because she was shot four times in the chest by her father-in-law and survived, the obvious inference that only homely baronesses would survive.

Enough! But a postscript: The father-in-law shot two more times, missing, then in a snit, did himself in. Draw your own conclusions.

I concluded, as I have many times, that the combination of the French Quarter and this city's history provides an opportunity for embellishment that exists nowhere else. Why? Where else can you find a 10-block-by-12-block virtual museum with hundreds of bars and enough characters to fill every stool?

Where else can you find story after story, even if they are the greatest collection of misinformation, cowflop and rumors this side of Johnny Horton's recording of "The Battle of New Orleans"?

Where else can you find Paul Revere in drag in the middle of the day? Nowhere, that's where. I rest my case.

Ain't Dere No More:
Da Schwegmann's Shoppers Bar

November 30, 2001

When Benny Grunch was talking to the master of Germania

13

Hall Masonic Lodge before a concert there this summer, they got on the subject of the late, great Schwegmann's Shoppers Bar.

The master, who was not from here, did not understand, as a local would, and wanted to know if it was a health bar, a snack bar, a salad bar or what.

"I told him it was a bar bar, that they sold Schwegmann's Beer, which was brewed by Dixie Beer, there," said Grunch. The master could not believe it. A bar in a supermarket? No way. But truth can be stranger than fiction, especially in New Orleans.

Many a husband spent some quality time at the bar inside the supermarket chain while his wife pushed the cart around the store, making groceries. One man, so the story goes, had his retirement party at the bar in the Harvey store, sponsored by the elder John Schwegmann, as thanks for spending so much time there.

That bar and the demise of Schwegmann's and other New Orleans institutions such as McKenzie's bakery, Krauss Co., K&B, Maison Blanche and D.H. Holmes inspired Grunch to write a new Christmas song on his "Twelve Yats of Christmas" CD (which includes a Yats colorin' book).

Titled "And Schwegmann's Gone Away (Ain't Dere No More)," it's an adaptation of "Jingle Bells," which as we all know begins with, "Dashing through the snow in a one-horse open sleigh," the Grunch song begins . . .

Everybody cried
On the live eyewitness news
McKenzie's got closed down
'Cause a sink was all mildewed;
Well, they opened up again
But while I was in line
They all closed down, but I heard they're gonna
Open one more time.

Chorus:
Just hotels, just hotels
More are on the way

Mr. Bingle quit at the Carlton Ritz
Cause he couldn't reach the buffet-ay
Krauss is gone so you can't try on
No queen-sized lingerie
But whatcha gonna do with K&B
And Schwegmann's gone away.

"The idea was to do a Christmas song and never mention Christmas," Grunch said. "Mr. Bingle is mentioned but he sounds more like an employee."

I asked if perpetuating these institutions in song was therapy for the pain of their loss.

"No, it's not that deep," he said. "I don't have any anxiety about losing things and places. To me it's all in the present. It's like they're still here and obviously I like to sing about it and joke about it. And the people who remember them are still here.

"It's just part of me and part of my friends and acquaintances. The humor I find in it is that even though physically they're gone, people still give directions like they're still there – such as 'I live around the corner from where Beelman's gas station used to be on Maple Street.'

"Now if they were gone and nobody remembered or cared about them and said, 'What's this song about?' then I'd probably need some serious therapy. I'd seek professional help."

Benny Grunch and the Bunch in the past month just finished playing at what he calls "the full worldwide Chalmette tour." That included Wahoo's Marina Bar, Desi Romano's Sports Bar, Soco's and Harbor View.

"Christmas in Chalmette" (another cut on the CD) is a big deal in Chalmette, he said, just as "Oh Little Town of Destrehan" is popular upriver.

Teaming up with Grunch in his New Orleans R&B and rock 'n' roll band are guitarist Allen Poche and drummer Harry Ravain, both originally from Arabi. Ravain always tells the Chalmette crowds: "Remember, Benny Grunch and the Bunch are more than 65 percent from St. Bernard." Obviously it's 66 2/3, but it sounds more impressive the other way. Grunch is an Orleanian who went to St. Aloysius High School, which also "ain't dere no more."

Even though many of the long-gone landmarks are mentioned, including A&G's, McCrory's, Waterbury's, Dailey's (Sing along: "Tell Dailey's who you are and where you work, and how you want to pay; for happy easy credit shopping buy the Dailey's way!"), Godchaux's, Miller Wohl, Labiche's, Kreeger's and Kress's, the reaction Grunch gets to his song when he plays live is always the same.

"We take a break and they all come up and talk about all the places and tell you about some more places you left out. How come you didn't mention Marks Isaacs or Gus Mayer's? Well, like any song, there are constraints of time," he said. Not so on his new Web site: www.bennygrunch.com.

But luckily, the Schwegmann's bar made the cut:

Paw-paw shopped at Schwegmann's
Forty years or more
'Cause Schwegmann's had a bar-room
Right there in the store;
Paw-paw got some French bread
Then he hung around
He'd walk home with the shopping cart
So he wouldn't just fall down.

The Noo Awlins Driving Quiz

October 12, 1994

A newcomer to the New Orleans area called this week to describe what he thought was an outrageous traffic maneuver that he had never before encountered in any city he had lived in.

The gentleman went on to describe a perfectly executed U-turn from the middle lane of a famous avenue where "No Left Turn" is clearly marked. The avenue, of course, is Tulane Avenue, the "No

Left Turn" capital of the world.

"My good man," I told the caller, "this is New Orleans. In the driver's mind, he clearly did not make a left turn; he made a U-turn."

"But he made it from the middle lane," the man protested.

"At least it wasn't from the right line," I replied.

Welcome to New Orleans driving, my friend. Simply keep Rule No. 1 in mind. It clearly states: "There are no rules."

Some years back, we published a Noo Awlins driving quiz, and I was going to send it to the gentleman but I could not locate it. However, I feel confident I can recreate and update it.

1. The single most important requirement for driving in New Orleans is:

a) An unfulfilled desire to play bumper cars.

b) A car that stalls frequently or burns oil.

c) An expired brake tag.

d) A desire to live on the edge.

2. "No Left Turn" signs:

a) Outnumber stop signs 50-1.

b) Were erected by the WPA in the 1930s solely to give jobless Americans something to do.

c) Have all the validity of a deed to Arizona oceanfront property.

d) Should be ignored at all times.

3. A yellow or orange sign with large black letters means:

a) Yield.

b) Detour.

c) You're in front of a Popeyes Fried Chicken outlet. Place your order and move on, please.

4. You're traveling on a main artery and the caution light suddenly, almost inexplicably and certainly unfairly turns to red before you get there. A red light means:

a) You and six more cars behind you can make it if you floor it.

b) Fresh doughnuts are being baked at your local Tastee outlet.

c) It's Christmas Eve and Rudolph the Red-nosed Reindeer is flying below the cloud cover.

5. "License Apply For" is an old French term that, loosely translated, means:

a) Somebody probably once owned this car.

b) The tape deck found in this car is awesome.

c) This sign takes the place of a license plate and under the Napoleonic Code is valid for the life of the car.

6. Rearview mirrors are very important. Their most important function is:

a) To enable you to put on your makeup or see if your mascara is running.

b) To hang fuzzy dice or Mardi Gras beads from.

c) To see if the couple you're double-dating with is off to the submarine races in the back seat.

7. The hand signal most frequently used by New Orleans drivers is:

a) A driver's arm raised 90 degrees, bent from the elbow to indicate a right turn.

b) A driver's arm extended out the window parallel to the ground to indicate a left turn.

c) The middle finger of either hand flipped up to indicate appreciation of another driver's maneuver in traffic.

8. Turn signals in New Orleans:

a) Are used in a hobby occasionally practiced by bored drivers.

b) Like mufflers, taillights and headlights, are optional equipment.

c) Should be used only when you're midway through executing a turn so no one has time to react.

d) For convenience, can be left on permanently, if desired.

9. The best place to park in New Orleans is:

a) On any sidewalk where your car blocks pedestrian traffic, or in front of a driveway or fire hydrant.

b) When there is better than a 20 percent chance of rain, any neutral ground.

c) Is best left to creative minds.

d) If there are no sidewalks, neutral grounds or driveways available, double parking is permitted.

10. Horns are used:
a) At a traffic signal to get the driver in front of you moving. A good rule of thumb is to wait about a nanosecond after the light turns from red to green before blasting him.
b) Strictly for recreational purposes.
c) To get the attention of a hunk or a babe walking on a sidewalk.

11. You see a green light. A green light means:
a) Don't make a move. At least six or seven cars are going to fly by at high rates of speed before it's safe to proceed.
b) Take a deep breath, make sure your seat belt is buckled, your will's in order and proceed with extreme caution.
c) Be ultra-cautious. That green light you see may be a neon Dixie Beer sign and you may be inside a bar. Get a designated driver to take you home.

12. The biggest nuisances to drivers in New Orleans are:
a) Pedestrians.
b) Potholes.
c) Bicyclists.
d) Stop signs and traffic signals.

13. Which of the following is not allowed in New Orleans?
a) Stopping in traffic to talk to another driver or a pedestrian.
b) Tailgating.
c) Passing on the right, or if there is no right, the sidewalk.
d) Straddling the center line of a roadway.
e) None of the above.

14. "Common Courtesy":
a) Was a bad Myrna Loy movie from the 1930s.
b) Won the Preakness and the Belmont Stakes after losing the Kentucky Derby.
c) Is an abstract, idealistic concept that may be practiced on some streets in some city somewhere, but not here.

Bonus: When you approach a traffic light that is clearly mal-functioning and is blinking red or orange, you should:
a) Wonder what color is blinking on the opposite side.
b) Flip a coin to see if you should stop or go.

c) Check to see if there are any empty cans you need to flip out the window.

d) Do exactly what the guy in front of you does.

And have a nice day.

Seymore D. Fair, Where Are You?

June 23, 2004

It was a pretty simple concept and it was simply delicious – a bag of Fritos filled with chili and other toppings – and it was called the Petro.

When rummaging through a drawer the other day, I stumbled onto our season passes for the 1984 World's Fair, which opened up a floodgate of wonderful memories, including that Tex-Mex delicacy which I ate more than any other food at the fair.

An entertainment success and a financial disaster for most investors, the fair provided one of the best venues ever for people-watching, hanging out and laughing and talking. It was colorful, zany, entertaining and memorable. And it's hard to believe two decades have gone by since then.

If you attended, you undoubtedly have your own memories. Here are mine:

The flashy City Gate entrance was designed by Barth Brothers and it featured enormous buxom mermaids and alligators that took the term "eye-catching" to a new level. One day Joe Barth got a call from a man identifying himself as a plastic surgeon from Ochsner Hospital interested in studying the mermaids.

Barth dismissed it as a practical joke from one of his friends.

But when a team of doctors from Ochsner did indeed show up – with a videotaping crew – he was told it was all in the cause of breast reconstruction research. Barth was floored. They were legit.

One of the best places at the fair to cool off was Sheila's, the

Australian pub on Fulton Street. In front was "art" that caught your attention: a13-foot-tall kangaroo drinking a Foster's lager. The giant marsupial had been carved with a chainsaw from an Algiers cypress tree.

Inside, the tables were maps of Australia carved into wood, and guarding the entire scene was Lady Godiva, nude astride her horse. The bartenders called her "Sheila," Aussie slang for chick or dame, just as bloke and mate are slang for guys.

The entertainment at the amphitheater on the river was nothing short of world class: Liberace, the Four Tops, the Temptations, James Taylor, the Charlie Daniels band, the Ellis Marsalis family and . . . Willie Nelson, quite possibly the best concert I've ever seen. Hearing the strains of "Always on My Mind" with the backdrop of tugboats and paddlewheelers going by on the river is near the top of my list of fair memories.

The official name of the fair, the 1984 Louisiana World Exposition, never caught on with the locals. What did was the season pass.

With a season pass, you had unlimited access, an offer which many area residents used. You didn't feel cheated if you went only for a couple of hours, whereas if you paid for a single day admission, you felt as if you had to spend the entire day and get your money's worth.

The fair opened in May and closed in November. Among other problems – including ridiculously optimistic attendance projections – was the heat. August was bad and just when you thought it might be cooling off, September was worse and October was one of the hottest Octobers in history.

But at least that was good news for places like Jed's Lookout, the Miller Beer Garden and its oom-pah-pah bands, and Reunion Hall, where Pete Fountain held sway. Kids could cool off at the Kid Wash, a car wash for youngsters, and the Watergarden, where you could pull off your shoes and cool your feet in the pool.

And even if it didn't cool you off, the humongous pool at the Aquacade mentally made you feel cooler. Many a day I felt like jumping in, but absolutely not from one of the 95-foot-tall diving boards where precision stunt divers did their thing. There was also water ballet and synchronized swimming, which was the last thing I thought I'd get hooked on.

But I did.

The whimsical Wonderwall featured winged cherubs and flying angels, among other things, and wound its way through the fair. Like many of the other attractions, including the Centennial Plaza, it offered a totally different look at night. The lights came alive, adding to the magical mystique that, in my humble opinion, was architectural genius.

When the fair closed, people bought sections of the Wonderwall and if you drive around the city, you can spot remnants still surviving in front and back yards.

There was more: The Vatican Pavilion, with its depictions of religious scenes by the masters Raphael, El Greco and Carvaggio. The spectacular fountains at Centennial Plaza; and of course, Seymore D. Fair, the top-hatted, tuxedo-clad, second-lining pelican mascot.

If I could take one more spin on the Ferris wheel or one more ride on the monorail, I'd do it in a heartbeat

But I'd skip the gondola, because I got stuck over the river for about five nerve-wracking minutes that seemed like a lifetime.

And when I got off and was back on land, I said a prayer, took a deep breath . . . and went to visit Sheila.

Ya Gotta Love the New Orleans Work Ethic

August 18, 1999

Ever try to find somebody on Friday afternoon in New Orleans?

Allow me to answer that question with two more questions:

How come in U.S. history class we grew up studying about the Puritan work ethic instead of the New Orleans work ethic?

Could it be because "New Orleans work ethic" may be the ultimate oxymoron, surpassing even the standards by which oxymorons are measured, terms such as military intelligence, airline food and partially pregnant?

An oxymoron, of course, is a combination of terms that contradict each other or are mutually exclusive. It is generally sarcastic or moronic or both. For example, until last season, if an LSU fan were asked to give an example of an oxymoron, he would say: Tulane football. Conversely, a Tulane fan might answer: Baton Rouge culture.

Let's get back to the original question: Ever try to find somebody on Friday afternoon in New Orleans? You might as well pan for gold outside the Federal Reserve Bank during a thunderstorm. Orleanians worshipped Friday afternoons long before the term T.G.I.F. was even coined. Everyone in New Orleans, at least everyone who has been here for a while, knows the weekend begins at lunch on Friday. That's because New Orleans, for better or worse, is blessed or cursed with the "joie de vivre" and "laissez les bons temps rouler" mentality. Neither of these terms, loosely translated, means long hours and hard work pay off.

Trying to explain the mindset and personality of a city to an out-of-towner is never an easy task, especially in less than an hour. But that's exactly what I was asked to do this week in my own cynical way. Here's what I told him, my spin on things:

To begin with – with apologies to chronological history — the Puritans, with their stern outlook on life, penchant for hard work and grim countenances, fortunately did not settle here – they settled in New England where the weather suited their personalities. Instead, we got, among other cultures, the French, who liked parties, wine, food and debauchery. Not to mention gambling and Carnival.

That was a good start. A very good start.

We were lucky enough to have a variety of peoples and their cultures, for a variety of reasons, settle here. We have been called a gumbo city and we have been called a melting pot and neither can be denied. We are an ethnic mix put into a blender and set on frappe' years ago. And from each culture, we seem to have gleaned their most hedonistic traits. These traits translated into a more leisure culture and a slower and easier pace.

No one enjoyed leisure more than the Spanish – one of the cultures that observes the siesta — and they didn't exactly shy away from red wine themselves. From the Germans who settled here we obviously got our love for beer. From the British and Irish we got our affinity for taverns and pubs, a fondness for sports like boxing and horseracing, and from the Italians, a deep love for food and music. More important, with the Irish and the Italians came St. Patrick's Day and St. Joseph's Day, which have now been combined into a virtual week-long street party.

Are you with me?

The English-speaking people who did settle in this general area, especially the wealthy, were more interested in doing things like racing horses and going on fox hunts than putting in a full day at the plantation. These people, even the less wealthy, were more pastoral, outdoor types and set aside time to go hunting and fishing. So very early on, priorities were set.

And when the Acadians arrived here after getting the heave-ho from Nova Scotia, they settled in the bayou areas where through the years they perfected the notion that you could paddle away your troubles and pass a good time fishing and cooking and partying. There were no license plates for horses, but the term "Sportsmen's Paradise" certainly applied. The Cajuns came to be known as one of the most fun-loving cultures anywhere and their food and music, never far from New Orleans, found a second home here.

The Caribbean and African black people who wound up here provided more cultural diversity and their food and music meshed in wonderfully. Some years down the road, their arrival would lead to jazz, always and forever the musical heart and soul of New Orleans and the French Quarter. Nightclubs and music, Storyville and the Big Easy — some more of our history. And a few short years later, this jazz would manifest itself in the form of an enormous two-week celebration hardly conducive to hard work. This would come to be known as Jazzfest. Music and food all day, all night for two consecutive extended New Orleans weekends.

They would also contribute one of the most mystical and intriguing concoctions known to man, the delicacy of gumbo, a spicy dark brown stew full of okra, seafood, chicken, sausage and file' — with as many versions as ingredients. Like the city's residents, it's an incredible mix.

And as many of those residents know, gumbo is a good lunchtime starting point on the way to disappearing on a Friday afternoon. Just don't forget to turn off your cell phone.

Nothing August About August

August 27, 1982

How do I hate thee, August? Let me count the ways.

This may take a while. When it comes to months that never should have been, August is in a class by itself. Without a doubt, it is the septic tank of the months of the year in New Orleans.

First, the obvious. August is hot, humid, muggy and miserable. It rains every afternoon. You stagger around the yard to cut the grass on Saturday, you sweat, you curse, you swat mosquitoes and gnats, and what do you get for a reward? On Monday it needs cutting again.

Your electric bill is higher than your house note. There are no holidays in August. New movies don't open in August. All you think about is staying inside hunkered down against the air conditioner or getting the hell out of town. There's no such thing as a cold shower in August. Even your swimming pool is hot in August.

Oh, sing a song of August, tra-la, tra-la . . . You can't – there aren't any. No songs or poems were ever written about August. No lyricist in his right mind would denigrate his reputation by eulogizing this miserable month. Besides, they're all out of town, swilling down frozen daiquiris by a cool stream, trying to remember the month of September.

School starts in August. Tuition fees are due in August. The

Cubbies have been mathematically eliminated in August. I went to basic training in the Army in August.

Hitler took over in August. The A-bomb was dropped on Hiroshima and Nagasaki. The yellow fever epidemic broke out in New Orleans. Hurricane Camille hit the Gulf Coast in 1969. Wild Bill Hickok was shot in the back with aces and eights in his hand in August. Marilyn Monroe, Elvis Presley, Will Rogers, Wiley Post and Rocky Marciano all died in August. Even Macbeth went on his tear in August.

The Berlin Wall was erected in August. Jack the Ripper claimed his first victim in August. PT-109 was sunk by a Japanese destroyer in August. The Mona Lisa was stolen from the Louvre in August. Even the immortal Man O' War lost his only race in August, beaten by a horse named Upset.

August ought to be cancelled, declared an intolerable abomination. Go straight from July to September. Start a citizens against August campaign. Re-name it. August is a total disaster, obviously designed to bake the brain and test one's spirit.

To add insult to injury, August is the most misnamed month of the year. August means "marked by majestic dignity or grandeur" and is named for the emperor Augustus Caesar. There is nothing majestic about August. As far as dignity, August is beneath anyone's.

There are fewer notations about August in Bartlett's book of quotes than any other months. Simon and Garfunkel years ago recorded a song about love entitled "April, Come She Will." What happens in August? August, die she must. Even if any desperate poet would want to, August is virtually impossible to rhyme.

August has the smallest file of any of the months in the newspaper morgue. In October, there are countless stories about pumpkins and Halloween. November is chock full of Thanksgiving and turkey recipes. December is fraught with holiday stories and Santa Claus. July is laden with historical celebration stories. February is Mardi Gras. April and May are dominated by Jazz Fest. August is zilch.

About 50 years ago, some deranged and misguided editorial writer, his mind obviously suffering from heat malfunction, pound-ed out an editorial entitled "Acres of August." I tried to read it. I stopped after "There is no ebb of purpose in the landscapes of August. Garden flower and leaf are as fresh as earliest morning air and new as the hours."

What was he smoking? Show me an August day with fresh early morning air and I will show you an August day in Antarctica.

I am trying to think of some good things to say about August. August is not any longer than the longest month of the year – it has only 31 days in it. When August arrives, it's a year until it gets here again. Nixon resigned in August. I usually go to a lobster party in August. The Saints season is close to starting.

And, oh yes, I got married in August. I'll never forget that night. The Saints lost to Buffalo, 24-21, in an exhibition game.

(As if that month didn't have a bad enough history, Hurricane Katrina in 2005 moved to the top of the list of events and things that have affected August's reputation.)

Big Bend: The Perfect Refuge From Katrina

August 30, 2006

The day I got married, the days my two children were born and August 28-29, 2005 – three of the happiest, most joyous days of my life and two days that were exhausting, confusing, terrifying, tragic and sad, eventually leading to the ruin of my city and uncertainty that is still with us today.

The story's been told, re-told, is being told and will continue to be told for generations as New Orleans rebuilds and rebounds. As World War II was for many, for New Orleans area and Gulf Coast residents who lived through the peril of Hurricane Katrina, it will always be a defining moment in their lives.

But today I leave that story to others and attempt to lighten things up through my own adventurous and amusing evacuation to a rural farmhouse no city kid like me was prepared to deal with.

I think about this a good deal, because in the midst of all the turmoil and anguish last September, this large block of fertile farmland on Bayou des Glaises in Avoyelles Parish – at a slow-paced blip on the map named Big Bend — brought peace, relaxation, and most importantly – laughter – into my life.

It also brought crowing roosters and mooing cows in the morning, singing birds and attack wasps during the day, while the sounds of crickets, frogs and other critters put you to bed at night. And stars like you never see in the city except when Katrina turned the lights out.

A lifetime buddy, William Marshall of Folsom, called the morning of August 28 and invited my wife and me to evacuate to his mom's rambling old farmhouse that hadn't been occupied on a regular basis since 1993. The place was equipped with some of the latest 1930s technology, such as a wood-burning stove to provide heat in the winter and some newer amenities like space heaters.

Called the old Blakewood home by some nearby residents of Bordelonville, Moreauville and Cottonport, the original house was built in the 1870s but the Great Flood of 1927 washed it away along with lives, livestock, homes, railroads, steamboats and everything in sight. The levee broke in those three communities and also Big Bend – which decades later prompted Randy Newman to record "Louisiana 1927."

The house was rebuilt in 1930 with more bedrooms than you could count and bunk beds to host large family gatherings.

After a grueling, circuitous, 12-hour, 293-mile drive that included a 16-mile, three-hour crawl on the Causeway, and an insane route that could have been plotted only by Cabeza de Vaca on his worst day with Jose Cuervo as his chief navigator, we put our heads down on an old four-poster bed that somehow survived the 1927 flood . . .

And got a special treat. A black and white animal crawled under the house and sprayed his finest essence of skunk. Welcome to La. Hwy. 451 and Big Bend. The aroma was, ah, revolting – that's as good a word as any — but total exhaustion overcame the scent.

Amidst the odor there was what I call the "Miracle of Freon." There were four ancient window units the likes of which haven't been seen in years and miraculously, they all worked.

The next day, August 29, between listening to radio and television reports, we set mouse traps in the house and bagged four, the limit. My wife was overjoyed, as you can imagine. And there were more surprises to come – including the larger, furrier rodent cousin.

We were in the midst of cotton, soybean and other fields growing stuff that city folks can't identify and the farm equipment and pickup trucks on the highway far outnumbered cars – definitely John Deere and denim country. The nearest place to get serious groceries and household items was in Marksville, about 25 miles away.

And it was there, at Harvest Foods supermarket, that I met Carl, an employee, and figured it all out. Things like this don't happen in the city. Carl spotted me as an interloper and started making small talk. He was very friendly, smiled a lot, walked around the store with me and pointed out where everything I needed was located.

I told Carl I was so discombobulated that I had totally lost track of time, more than I ever had in my life. And then Carl, who came from a tiny Louisiana community that no longer exists, laughed, and imparted to me some great country wisdom that had been imparted to him:

"Time don't mean nuthin' to a hog," he said. I laughed out loud. In the days and weeks to come, I would find out that Avoyelles is hog country, and appreciate his philosophy even more.

In the evenings, we sat out on the large screen porch and had cocktails and watched the sun go down. Every couple of days, I would get in the car and drive to Marksville to restock the bar and get some health food like frozen pizza. A 50-mile round trip to buy beer, wine, etc., isn't normal in the city but with nothing to do and no place to go, well, time don't mean nuthin' to a hog.

Then one day, I stopped at a little store on the bayou that was only about three miles from the house because I had to refill the propane tank that heated the water in the house. They had a couple of old gas pumps and it looked like nothing more than a bait store from the outside.

I walked in and the first thing I saw was cooler after cooler of beer, wine racks and booze. They had a full deli and groceries. This big dummy had been driving 50 miles and here it was, an oasis only three miles away. The next thing you knew, they were special ordering New Orleans coffee with chicory for us.

The weeks there left me with memories I'll never forget. I'd see my name, "A. LIND 7464 HWY. 451", in large block letters on the roadside mailbox on the blacktop two-lane highway and shake my head in disbelief. It was exactly 160 yards from the door to the mailbox – I stepped it off one day – you do things like this with too much time on your hands.

And the address was a Moreauville address, not Big Bend or Bordelonville – they weren't big enough for a post office.

This I learned from the electrician we called. He was named Brian Bordelon. Well, Bordelonville – makes sense. The next day the TV guy came by. He was named Stacy Bordelon, some kind of cousin of Brian Bordelon.

I was lucky enough to meet my neighbor a couple of miles down the road, Bernadine "Bird" Laborde, a young 91-year-old who survived the Great Flood of 1927 and told me all about it between cocktails. She said the TV images of Katrina's floodwaters brought back her '27 memories, minus the cows swimming for their lives and the chickens on the rooftops.

We hung clothes on an old clothesline, which blowing in the wind became an amusement for the neighbor's playful Lab puppy, who liked to pull them down. Then I hooked up the dryer and the washer – at least two times – because I screwed it all up.

But my immediate neighbor, who was very handy, always came to my rescue when I was klutzing around.

We watched fuzzy images of the storm's aftermath on an old TV with rabbit ear antennas and aluminum foil wrapped around them. No CNN, FOX or ESPN for us until we got satellite TV a couple of weeks later. And you know what? It wasn't a big deal.

I never could understand why anyone would want to live in a small town. But after 42 days in Big Bend, it came to me:

People aren't uptight like they are in the city, the pace is slow and concern for your fellow man is high. There's no rat race, no road rage, no gridlock, no traffic jams, no traffic report, heck – there's no traffic. There's also no crime and no murders.

People lend a hand anytime. Nobody blows you off. Nobody is rude. Nobody's in a hurry. Everybody waves or says hello. That's all built into their makeup. If only the city were like that.

When we packed up and pulled out, we picked some cotton from a nearby field as a memento, and left some purple, green and gold Rex beads on a sideboard – oh, and some cold beer in the fridge for the next displaced souls that might seek refuge there.

As we passed Bird Laborde's place on the highway, I remembered her telling me that in Avoyelles Parish, the '27 flood has never been forgotten. "It is still talked about here, just like New Orleans will be doing with Katrina for years."

Then I turned on a CD and listened to Kermit Ruffins.

CHAPTER 2

The Legendary Characters

Dr. Momus Alexander Morgus

September 1, 1981

Churchill visited Ike and ate dinner at Bernard Baruch's house. Hawaii became the 50th state. Big-bucks TV quiz shows like "$64,000 Question" and "21" were exposed as fixed. Castro took over Cuba. The Dodgers beat the White Sox in the World Series, and the Pelicans folded after 72 years in the Southern Association. Miss Mississippi, Lynda Lee Mead, was named Miss America.

The year was 1959.

In New Orleans, a group named the Saxons was playing an 8 till 11 p.m. gig at a St. Anthony's school dance. At about 10:15 the place emptied, and one of the St. Anthony brothers walked up to the bandstand and told the Saxons to knock off, pack it in. "What are we doing wrong, Father?" one of the musicians asked.

"Nothing," said the priest. "They're all going home to watch Morgus."

In 1959 in New Orleans, a mad, mad scientist had called his bumbling assistant an idiot for the first of many, many times. The year marked the emergence of Morgus the Magnificent and his side-kick Chopsley as the slapstick co-hosts of WWL-TV's "House of Shock." With the zany but confused Dr. Morgus in semi-control of his experiments, the late-night horror film package took the city as few local shows ever have.

The song "Monster Mash" by Bobby Boris Pickett best described what happened: "They were a graveyard smash, they caught on in a flash."

Morgus had crazed eyes, an insufferable ego and a sinister laugh. He toiled in his Rube Goldberg laboratory over the Old City Ice House in the French Quarter, predicting great success for his experiments while he shuffled electrodes and test tubes.

His forte was incompetence. While the ghouls, werewolves and vampires were separating the men from the boys in the feature movie of the night, Morgus created such things as the Morgussal Perpetual Cardiomachine, guaranteed to make you live 200 years, and the Morgusso Incizo-machine. Designed to make the scalpel a thing of the past, it was a jigsaw for surgeons with shaky hands.

During commercial breaks in the movie, in six five-minute segments, Morgus would tell of the spectacular progress he was making and then, of course, the inevitable dismal failure of his undertakings (poor choice of words there, considering his many victims).

"Chopsley, you idiot! You paleologic moron!" was possibly one of the nicest bouquets that Sid Noel, as the comically ghoulish Dr. Morgus, ever tossed in the direction of massive 6-foot, 7-inch Tommy George. George, as Chopsley, lumbered around Morgus' laboratory in a black, hooded executioner's outfit and incapably assisted the master in his experiments. Chopsley was clumsy and incompetent. But his loyalty to Morgus was unquestioned.

The pair was on television in three decades: from '59 until the early '60s; again from '65 until sometime in '67; and for the third time on WDSU-TV in '70-'71.

When they formed their partnership, Noel was a radio personality for WWL and George was, ironically, a guitar player with the Saxons. It would be a long time before their real-life identities would be discovered.

Today, Noel, who now looks like a handsome Karl Malden, lives in St. Tammany Parish and is in business for himself.

George, who facially resembles John Mecom Jr., lives in Meraux, La. He was a motorcycle police officer with the St. Bernard Sheriff's Office until his retirement two years ago. As Chopsley, George never uttered a single word in all those years in front of the cameras. But it comes as no surprise that someone as tall and massively built as George has a voice so deep it makes Charles Kuralt sound like a soprano.

Both men have raised families and are exceptionally private people. They declined to have their photographs taken or discuss their personal lives, preferring to carry over the mystique that their anonymity on the show created.

But in spite of the fact that they have faded from the show business scene, for viewers who witnessed the master dropping test tubes, operating on gullible victims – usually Chopsley – and creating machines that fizzled and popped and smoked and eventually blew up, the memory of the days of the "House of Shock" will never dim.

"It's amazing," George said recently, shaking his head. "We're talking about a ten-year-old dead horse and people still want to know: When will it come back? All we had was a handful of the classics, the great horror movies. The rest were Grade Z Japanese movies. I don't know how we pulled it off."

But they did.

The Morgus saga began in 1958 when WWL-TV bought a package of horror films and began looking for a host. Noel, who had been dealt the tough chore of replacing the long-running Dawnbusters show on radio, tried out for the job. He won out over many rivals, including a former member of Our Gang comedies. "If I do it," he recalled telling Channel 4 programmers, "it's going to have to be funny. You can only say 'Boo!' once or twice." Noel also wanted no identity with the show.

Morgus was seen briefly by himself before Chopsley got into the act. That came about when George entered a Horror Hop costume contest at Municipal Auditorium and won it as Count Dracula. The rumor was that the winner was supposed to get a guest shot on Morgus' show, but that never came to pass. Meanwhile, Morgus made a guest appearance at a sock hop in Bay St. Louis. The two rode home together and one thing led to another.

Noel had as much fun creating Morgus as Dr. Frankenstein did putting life into his monster. He decided that the Morgus concept should have three elements: 1) The display of an ego that never quit; 2) A satirical look at the world of science and the shortcomings of academia; and 3) A focus on the bottom rung of humanity – the common man, poverty level.

Morgus was a lot more complicated than his fans realized. Innuendos and potshots at society were as much a part of his game as gamma rays and neutrons. His real name was Momus Alexander Morgus: for Momus, the god of ridicule; Alexander the Great, the biggest egomaniac in history; and Morgus, a blend of morgue and disgusting.

Noel took the ball and ran with it.

"Can you imagine somebody giving you a stage to create a character?" he recalled recently. "I wanted to sculpture him just like an artist would. It was a real chance to impart some social thought. There were references to conditions we were all caught up in . . . electric bills rising, for example."

Typical of the times, Morgus wouldn't take a federal grant for his lab. He proudly wore his filthy lab coat. Each stain, he would say, was a monument to one of his experiments. He strove for recognition by "those of the university who ostracize me." He liked to remind viewers of the many books he had written, including "Protons I Have Known," "Brain Surgery – Self Taught," and his classic, "New Hope for the Dead."

"We are all a bunch of Morguses anyway," Noel laughed, "faking it, fooling everybody, with self-serving egos."

Morgus criticized everybody from The Times-Picayune to Mayor Moon Landrieu. He was always at war with society and often commented: "I never met a molecule I liked." If Morgus were around today, Mayor Dutch Morial would really be in hot water.

The master was always miffed because none of the city's landmarks were named after him. At the time he suggested that the 17th Street Canal be renamed the Morgus Canal. "So what if it's a drainage canal? It carries the sweat of my labors," he said.

Morgus tried to beat the phone company, stole electricity from his neighbor and when NOPSI sent him a bill anyway, he was incensed. "How could they send us a bill, Chopsley? We don't even use their electricity!"

"He was not the magnificent," said Noel. "He was a social thesis. I was into all of this back then. I was a liberal, not in every sense, but I was concerned for the environment, the Sputnik thing." Morgus had a bent posture and stooped shoulders. On the back of his lab coat was a bloody handprint, a symbol of life pushing him down.

"I was looking for every symbol back then," Noel recalled. "I was a symbol freak. Morgus used Chopsley just as corporations and businesses and government use the masses – as guinea pigs."

Morgus was always trying to get Chopsley to be the victim. Chopsley would protest, then get sucked in one more time. "I promise you, you won't feel a thing," he would tell poor Chopsley.

Occasionally, Morgus would realize that his henchman resented his authority, a knowledge that would really bring his ego to the fore. "Some of us are born to serve, Chopsley, and some of us are born to command. Was it Aristotle who said that – or was it I?"

When Chopsley threw the wrong switch or failed to follow instructions, it was: "How can you be around me so much and know so little? Ah, fools can only get by so long, Chopsley, you idiot!"

Poor Chopsley took a lot of abuse but Morgus would occasionally throw him a backhanded compliment. "Yes, Chopsley, heh-heh, I will admit you have one big advantage over me – you are in better company than I am."

He even explained on one show exactly why he called him an idiot. IDIOT – it stood for "inability demonstrated in organizing thought." Then he glowered at Chopsley and said, "Half the idiots out there don't even know they're idiots."

George, an avowed horror movie freak long before the Morgus era, even went so far as to forge his own executioner's axe. It was no lightweight prop. He cut it out of half-inch plate steel and designed the costume after researching exactly what executioners wore. He worked to perfect Chopsley's shuffling movements and his ominous presence. "If you left him alone and didn't antagonize him, he wouldn't bother you," George said. But his size and appearance made him quite a specter to unsuspecting guests in the laboratory.

Also playing off Morgus' gigantic ego was Eric the skull, whose voice was that of Ed Hoerner, probably most recently known for his appearances at dinner theaters.

"Eric was what we all need," said Noel. "A yes man." Anytime Morgus needed confidence, he would ask Eric and Eric would say, "Yes, master." Eric introduced and closed the show ("Good night, master") backed up by the eerie music made by turning a frequency oscillator up and down.

The lab set was makeshift but adequate for those days in television. The bubbles in the vials and the smoke that came from them were provided by a lot of dry ice from the Pelican Ice Company. On Morgus' walls from time to time would appear such signs as: "Fight Mental Health," "Stop Breeding," "Help Kill Welfare . . . WORK," "Your Organ Donations Are Tax Deductible."

The early shows were live, and the viewers weren't the only ones surprised. One night, for some reason, a Western movie was shown instead of the usual horror movie. Morgus liked to follow story plots in his lab, so he did a takeoff on it. None other than "Bad" Masterson was coming to town, he told his audience, and Morgus was going to fix Chester's limp and who knows what all. The Jefferson Parish sheriff's deputies were chasing some Indians, who attacked Morgus' lab.

On the set at WWL-TV, Noel was outfitted with a metal shield and a six-inch piece of foam. When the camera moved away, a prop man shoved an arrow into his protected back. But Morgus once zigged when he should have zagged, and the prop man promptly shoved an arrow into his ribs. They weren't play arrows. And he couldn't cry out or the scene would have been ruined.

"We were live," Noel said. "You get mixed emotions when something like that happens. It's like seeing your mother-in-law drive off a cliff in your Cadillac." He had to get a tetanus shot.

On another occasion, Arthur Jones of "Wild Cargo" provided Morgus witn a 13-foot alligator presumably tranquilized. The premise for this show was that Morgus would take a common lizard, inject it with one of his famous Morgussal serums and transform it into a full-sized gator. Several iguanas of varying sizes were bought from pet stores so that the lizard could grow gradually during the intermissions.

When the alligator was unveiled, Chopsley walked over to him. The alligator promptly whomped him across the thigh with his tail, tore his trousers and put a large welt on his leg. It also knocked him over into the set.

This was not a banner show for Chopsley. Morgus had a ceiling fan over his operating table. Just for a nice touch, they put a six-foot live snake up there so the reptile could stick its head down from time to time and bother Morgus.

Morgus finally told Chopsley to get rid of the snake, and when George approached, the snake struck him. The stunned actor pulled away so fast that he ripped all of the snake's fangs and teeth out of his head. "I got bit good," he said.

One futuristic touch to the show took place on the night the master created Morgus clones. "And that was 20 years ago," said Noel. "You know, 'M*A*S*H' is a modern Morgus, a typical situation of what is really going on – people with serious obligations screwing up all the time – the old 'a little knowledge is a dangerous thing' syndrome."

The show was hot. Letters poured into WWL-TV. Famous names, in disguise, made appearances: Steve Allen, Tiny Tim, Mike Douglas, Marty Allen. Even hizzonner, Vic Schiro, made a guest shot.

Plans were made for the appearance of another guest but were never carried out: The proposed script called for Morgus to decide that he was going to use the sewers of the city to air condition New Orleans. The city was to find out about it and Morgus was to suspect that his lab was bugged. The show was to have ended with Morgus pulling off Chopsley's hood and finding behind it another large man – District Attorney Jim Garrison.

"I talked to Garrison about it later," chuckled Noel, "and he laughed and swore he would have done it at the time."

Morgus fever grew wild. The movie made in 1961, "The Wacky World of Dr. Morgus," was shown on Halloween of 1980 and the theater was packed. Airplane pilots reported that they could see the lights in New Orleans homes go off at 10:30 p.m. when the show was on. Superintendent of Police Joe Giarrusso even told Noel once that the crime rate dropped noticeably during Morgus' time slot.

A couple of years after the show began, WWL-TV sportscaster Hap Glaudi unthinkingly blew Noel's cover. Glaudi simply wanted to compliment Noel on the show's huge success, but it never dawned on him that the anonymity was important.

"It was the kind of thing," George recalled, "where everybody knew Morgus' name was Sid Noel, the announcer on WWL radio. That was easy enough. Years later, though, they found out about Tommy George. Well, who is Tommy George? Well, he's the guy who plays Chopsley, that's all. No big deal."

Only George's fellow musicians knew his identity and Noel's face was not really identifiable as that of a wacky scientist. Noel recalls getting a ride from the radio station to the TV station in a cab one day and the cabbie saying, "WWL-TV, huh? That's the station that creep Morgus is on."

Noel drifted off to Detroit between the first and second runs here, after a disagreement with WWL over public appearances, and he tried playing Morgus up there. George went to broadcast school in New York in the interim. The pair was reunited after things were smoothed over and the show was a hit again.

But for one reason or another, it went off the air again in '67. When it was revived for a '70-'71 run, the show was on WDSU in the afternoon, the wrong time slot. While some of those shows were the best technically, things weren't quite the same in the afternoon.

Then in 1971, while still shooting Morgus, officer Tommy George was struck by an automobile on Paris Road while escorting a funeral on his motorcycle. He slid 147 feet down the highway and his shattered leg was pinned under his cycle. He lay in muddy water until an ambulance arrived, and subsequently contracted a dirt germ infection that has remained a problem for 10 years, through many operations. It prevents healing and flares up from time to time.

At about the same time, Sid Noel decided he had enough of being Morgus. He had always maintained outside business interests and was ready to give them a try. "You can't keep topping yourself.

I figured I had gone as far as I would go. The TV and radio medium is like a fickle mistress. I knew that a long time before. I just decided the time had come."

So in 1971, Morgus called Chopsley an idiot for the last time. But the memory lingers.

"If people want to see Morguses today, all they have to do is look around them," says Noel. "They're everywhere. People dumping poisonous wastes into the river and then trying to convince people there's no harm. You can see a Morgus and you can see a Chopsley.

"Did I enjoy it? . . . It was like being on a float every week, like the characters who pay thousands of dollars to hide behind masks in Carnival organizations. Of course I did."

Tommy George's fires burn stronger. "The curiosity is still there. Strange things have been happening, man . . . strange things," he adds with a tone of Morgussal mystery. "I wonder if I know about it all."

"Would it go in the '80s? Absolutely. I don't think time has anything to do with it. What made the thing play was that Noel knew what I thought and I knew what he thought. He was the first one that I know of to combine horror and comedy. To my knowledge that has never been done before."

People may indeed ask: Why not again?

And with that: "Good night, master."

(Sid Noel is alive and well on the Northshore. Morgus still toils in his lab above the Old City Icehouse. Tommy George is deceased.)

Black Cat: A Case of the Shorts

November 7, 2000

When Jimmie Davis, the always and forever "You Are My Sunshine" singing governor of Louisiana, died this week at 101, it brought back some funny memories of the 1959 gubernatorial campaign as told by one of Davis' adversaries in that race, the legendary Allen "Black Cat" LaCombe.

A racetrack handicapper and publicist, boxing promoter extraordinaire, con artist, rogue and ultimate Irish Channel character, LaCombe had moved with his family to New Orleans from Echo, La. He jumped in the 1959 race against Davis and seven others on a dare from the bar rats at Curley's Neutral Corner. That, like Raymond's Beach, was a sporting establishment for boxing fans, bookies and racetrackers located on Poydras Street.

Proprietor Curley Gagliano sponsored the $250 qualifying fee for the Black Cat plus a double sawbuck for the bus ride to Baton Rouge to file his papers. There were some heavyweights in this campaign, including another former governor, James A. Noe, former New Orleans Mayor Chep Morrison, and former state auditor Bill Dodd.

Davis was a colorful major figure in Louisiana's storied political history, doing more singing than politicking — but LaCombe was one of the finest supporting actors. As my late friend Bob Krieger, one of local TV's finest humorists, observed, "Black Cat was the perfect candidate for governor – and that was long before Edwin Edwards."

LaCombe delighted in reliving his "campaign" years later, but every time he did so the circumstances and figures were a little different. But the tale was so good, the "news guys," as LaCombe called reporters, overlooked that. They never let the facts interfere with a good story. He would tell Iris Kelso one version, Mel Leavitt another, Bob Roesler and Pete Finney still one more and have a new spin on it when I checked in.

He said he figured he would run pretty well even though his campaign suffered from "a case of the shorts," or no money. Most of LaCombe's life he suffered from the "shorts," but it never changed his upbeat personality and his belief that a longshot would run in tomorrow and he would be rich. His reasoning was that he was on the ballot between top contenders Davis and Morrison and a lot of people would make mistakes pulling the lever.

His plan was to hitchhike the state, and he did make it to Echo, his birthplace, which is a small central Louisiana town near Marksville in Avoyelles Parish. He predicted he would carry Echo because most of the people there were related to him. He asked voters for their vote, a cup of coffee and a ride to the next town. He said he chose that method of campaigning because of "severe financial stress."

He also told voters that the smarts were predicting that no one could win in the first primary. "Now ladies and gentlemen," he said, "this means your vote doesn't mean too much in the first primary, no matter who you vote for. So if you're going to throw your vote away, please throw it my way."

As it turned out, Davis won but the campaign trail turned into a mini-gold mine for Black Cat. He got to talking to Jimmy Noe one night; Noe asked him how he was doing and LaCombe told his tale of financial woe again. So, one version of the story goes, when they shook hands, Noe, a wealthy radio mogul, greased LaCombe's palm with four C-notes.

"Lawd, look at dis angel, straight from heaven. Gawd musta sent me dis," he told Iris Kelso years later. Mel Leavitt heard a slightly different version, but what happened afterwards was this: LaCombe followed Noe wherever he went and told voters to vote for someone who can win. There were more handshakes and more hundred dollar bills changed hands. "The most generous guy I ever met," LaCombe would say.

He finished seventh in a field of nine, "up the track," as Allen himself would tell you, but it didn't matter. He wound up in a chapter in one of the most famous books ever written about Louisiana politics, A.J. Liebling's "The Earl of Louisiana."

In February of 1987, a bunch of "news guys" threw a party at the Fair Grounds honoring Black Cat, whose health was fading. It was basically to thank him for all the years making them laugh. The ticket for "Black Cat Fun Night" cost $13, a rather appropriate amount. One of the greatest collections of this town's Runyonesque characters turned out and the stories were told and retold.

There was a giant banner hanging overhead that said, "LaCombe for Governor." There was another with one motto: "Run the squirrels out of office – keep the state safe for the nuts." And across the way was another: "Use your dome – vote for LaCombe!" His "platform" included a four-day work week, the return of big-time boxing and promotion of honest sports, such as wrestling; a ceiling of $150 for campaign expenses, and a pledge to give race-horses two days off a week from training, just like everybody else.

Jimmie Davis went around the state singing his songs, playing his guitar, and eventually wound up on the Grand Ole Opry in Nashville. He left us fairly traditionally this week, in a conservative ceremony.

Black Cat's departure started traditionally, from P.J. McMahon's parlor, but it wound up with his Cadillac hearse taking a spin around the one-mile Fair Grounds oval.

At the finish line, the hearse stopped and the bugler blew "Taps," followed by every racetrackers' favorite song, the "Call to the Post." We knew we were saying good-bye to an incredible character.

And now, Jimmie Davis has ridden his horse into the sunset, marking the end of an era of colorful politics that was amusing and didn't hurt anybody.

Leapin' Lou: The Ultimate Promoter

January 10, 1986

It was August of 1975 when Leapin' Lou Messina made his pitch to the Superdome Commission.

"You name it – we'll promote it," the irrepressible boxing promoter told the slightly bewildered panel. Messina had put together an unlikely group called "Productions Unlimited," which included Allen "Black Cat" LaCombe, Joe Gemelli, Tex Stevens, Ed Cocke, Jack Dempsey and Don Kern. He then passed out to the commission members some brochures which contained the following information:

43

"We specialize in conventions, world championship boxing shows, trade shows, beauty pageants, football, baseball, basketball games, rodeos, rock and roll and country western shows, jazz concerts, camel races, Carnival balls, opera, ballet."

Boxing shows? No doubt about it. Camel races? Maybe. But opera and ballet? No way. If Lou Messina told you he was going to New York to see Carmen, the Carmen he was talking about was Carmen Basilio – and the performance would take place in a ring at Madison Square Garden. If you had asked him about Broadway, the only Broadway he knew was Broadway Johnny the Fox Cox, one of the rather unconventional cronies he hung out with down at Raymond's Beach, a watering hole of note once located at the corner of Poydras and St. Charles.

Lou Messina died this past Monday, leaving the world of sports with a void that will never be filled. Old-time boxing promoters have been on the endangered species list for years, and they are fast becoming extinct. Messina, LaCombe, and the late Curley Gagliano, proprietor of Curley's Neutral Corner, for decades were the Barnum and Bailey plus one of local boxing, operating out of the old Coliseum Arena and the Municipal Auditorium.

"You hadda like him," said LaCombe, the last of the Mohicans. "He was the best summabitch you ever saw. We were partners for 50 years, from the first day we met. Well, we weren't exactly partners – I didn't put up no money."

Those who knew what made Leapin' Lou tick would tell you that wouldn't make any difference. He was the eternal optimist, always convinced that the next fight would produce the pot of gold at the end of the rainbow. He also believed that this was the greatest fight town in America, and boxing was forever making a comeback.

No doubt Messina set the record for promoting more "fights of the century" in the same century than any man in history. If it wasn't the fight of the century, than it was the Deep South junior middleweight title bout, or some other grandiose but unofficial billing that he and the Black Cat conjured up.

And although he was responsible for countless championship

boxing cards, and brought in either as fighters or guest referees such big names as Basilio, Rocky Marciano, Sugar Ray Robinson, Willie Pastrano, the Docusen brothers, Ralph Dupas, Willie Pep, Joe Brown, Sandy Sadler, Bob Foster and Jimmy Perrin, the big payoff always seemed to elude him.

"I've always been the publicity man – maybe that was the problem," said LaCombe. "He lost a ton of money, I know that. We had some tough days. His main problem was his heart was too big. Anybody around him who was busted or broke, if he had a dollar, he gave it to 'em. He fed me many a day when I was hungry, gave me money when I was broke."

Of course, there were hefty big paydays between the sob stories. Otherwise, there wouldn't be pictures of Leapin' Lou all smiles in the newspaper files. There's one in which he's carrying a big suitcase of money on the way to the bank after the welterweight fight between Percy Pugh and Jerry Pellegrini in 1966. In that one, Messina admitted to making "a few bucks." But he was forever known as "Break Even" Louie because of the never-changing financial disclosure statement he made following each fight he promoted. "We broke even" was his standard.

His more famous nickname he never could shake. "Leapin' Lou" was there to stay after he literally leapt into the ring to stop the Cosby Linson-Johnny Greco fight in 1952. The wrong boxer, Linson, was winning, and Messina's visions of a rematch were going up in smoke. There is an asterisk next to his leap that explains that it was aided by John Barleycorn. In his clouded mind he figured that if he stopped the fight before a decision was rendered, he could stage a rematch. Indeed, there was a rematch. But it was in Montreal, and Messina wasn't the promoter – he had been suspended by the state boxing commission.

Messina once described the strangest fight he ever witnessed, and for a man who saw as many fights as he did, you'd have to believe it. Two bantamweights, Jock Leslie and a Mexican named Pee Wee Flores, were fighting. Both were stiff punchers, and Flores was a southpaw. In an early round, they both let fly with haymakers. Incredibly, both connected. Flores hit the deck and never moved. But so did Leslie.

The count began. Leslie managed to pull himself to his feet as the count reached nine. He collapsed a couple of seconds later, but was declared the winner because he beat the count – although only for a second.

Messina wanted to be laid out in a boxing ring at Municipal Auditorium. He got the idea from Tex Rickard, the promoter of the Dempsey-Tunney fight, who was waked in Madison Square Garden. At the side of Messina's casket at Lamana-Panno-Fallo was a concession to his wishes: a floral spray in the shape of a boxing ring.

Among the fight crowd gathered to say goodbye were Mike Cusimano and Otis Guichet, Jerome Conforto and Charley Joseph, and way too many others to name. LaCombe pushed his way through the crowd to see Messina's sons, Lou and Charlie. "If we'da had this many people for some of those matches, we'da never broke even," said LaCombe. "We'da made a ton of money."

"My dad had a real full life," Charlie Messina said.

Indeed he did. To steal a line that was written about Bill Veeck, the roguish baseball impresario who died last week, the cause of Messina's death, like Veeck's, should be listed as: too much life.

Ol' Uncle Earl: The Last of the Red Hot Poppas

April 11, 2003

The year was 1959 and Uncle Earl Long, the three-time good ol' country boy governor of the great state of Louisiana, had lost a hard-fought battle for lieutenant governor on the Jimmy Noe ticket. After that and on into 1960, he was campaigning for the Eighth U.S. Congressional District seat held by incumbent Harold McSween.

Somewhere in the country near Leesville, approaching the community of Hicks, Long's black Mercury was speeding along when he suddenly ordered his chauffeur to stop and turn into a driveway leading to an old double-wide shotgun farm house. The family recognized Long immediately and invited him in for coffee. While they were talking he spotted an old Dominicker hen and her seven little chicks.

Uncle Earl asked in his gravely voice, "How much you want for that old Dominicker hen and her biddies? I been wanting one just like that for my Pea Patch farm up in Winnfield."

The couple told the governor to please take them but Long said no way, paid them $7.50, put them in his car and went on his way. Some miles down the road, Uncle Earl ordered the driver to suddenly stop again. The same scene was pretty much repeated from the previous stop. Uncle Earl talked politics, then told that family, "I've brought you something from my Pea Patch farm up in Winnfield."

He instructed Jay Chevalier to go to the car and get the Dominicker hen and her brood and give them to the family. Chevalier, a handsome young country singer, was stumping around the state on the campaign trail with Uncle Earl, singing "The Ballad of Earl K. Long," a monster hit that he had written before he even met Long.

Chevalier brought the hen and her chicks to the family, which was thrilled to have an authentic hen and chicks from the governor's farm.

"It was genius," Chevalier was saying this week from his Kenner home, where he lives with wife Gisela and a talking cockatiel named Lucky. "In five miles he picked up 200 votes, maybe more, for seven bucks. Those people would tell those stories to their friends and kinfolks who would tell them to other friends and kinfolks for years to come. And they would all vote for him."

It was old-fashioned politicking back then. Uncle Earl's car was always full of hams, frozen turkeys, tomatoes, okra, corn, beans and other vegetables and fruit, all allegedly from his beloved Pea Patch farm. He doled them out to people wherever he stopped to have a rally and stump. And in the middle of it all for 13 surreal, sometimes tragicomic months was 23-year-old Chevalier, a singer with a slicked-back pompadour from outside Forest Hill, La., population 492 – whose only dream was to become a top country singer.

Chevalier has written a book, "Earl K. Long and Jay Chevalier: When the Music Stopped." It is a book Chevalier, now 67, calls "a labor of love." He still shakes his head in disbelief that this actually happened to him – that his life became so entwined with one of this state's legendary characters, Earl K. Long.

The book, published by Southern Legacies Press, comes with Chevalier's CD, "Lost in Louisiana 1959."

"As far as I'm concerned, 1959 was the last great year in Louisiana," said Chevalier. "LSU was number one in the college football polls. Billy Cannon won the Heisman Trophy. The Louisiana Hayride in Shreveport was still going strong, producing stars like Elvis, Johnny Cash, Kitty Wells and Faron Young. The CMA (Country Music Association) was born that year and down in New Orleans, Cosimo Matassa was the focal point, recording guys like Fats Domino, Chuck Berry and Little Richard."

And Chevalier was part of Uncle Earl's entourage, hired entertainment that warmed up the crowd with barkers and frontmen. Before Long left the governor's mansion, Chevalier had his own personal room there, his own room at the Roosevelt Hotel in New Orleans, the Bentley Hotel in Alexandria and the Pentagon Barracks in Baton Rouge. He had become part of Uncle Earl's inner circle.

"I was just dazzled by him. I had never been around anyone that magnetic," he said. "I had just come out of the Marine Corps, so he was my commandant, my commander-in-chief. He was the last of the great stump speakers and the last of the red hot poppas."

At the time Long was estranged from his wife Blanche and it was no secret he was deeply involved with the star of Bourbon Street, the Sho-Bar's red-headed stripper Blaze Starr.

"I think Blaze loved him. A lot of his relatives don't want to hear that," said Chevalier. "She was making thousands a week. She didn't need the power, she didn't need an old man."

Long would show up at the Sho-Bar with the same routine. He gave away vegetables and told them it came from the Pea Patch. "They came from the Schwegmann's on Airline," said Chevalier.

"But it worked. Everywhere he went, it was feeding the multitudes, the Jesus technique. Everybody came to Uncle Earl's rallies because they knew they were going home with something."

Noe and Long didn't make the runoff. The baggage of having been in two mental institutions and some of the crazy stunts Uncle Earl pulled, like buying bullwhips and cowboy hats and giving them away, not to mention peeing in a flowerpot at the Roosevelt Hotel and streaking down a hallway, had caught up with him.

Long never denied being crazy. In fact, it produced one of his best campaigning lines. When people sided with Blanche's contention that he was crazy, Long would say: "They say I'm crazy. Well, if I'm crazy now, I was crazy then, and if I was crazy then, then I've been crazy all of my life and some of you must be crazy too 'cause you voted for me three or four times."

After the defeat, Chevalier was devastated. But not long after that, Uncle Earl announced he was running for the Eighth Congressional District seat and dreams of Washington, D.C. danced in his head. At every stop, in places like Cheneyville, Uncle Earl would refer to his incumbent opponent as "Catfish-Mouth" McSween. The road show started up all over again.

And guess what? He won. That was the good news. The bad news is that he died of a heart attack 11 days after he was elected.

"He was stubborn and persistent but he was such a captivating figure. Everybody has an Uncle Earl and I story," said Chavalier. "I've only seen four or five people in person that would set a building on fire with electricity – Elvis Presley, Edwin Edwards, Maurice Chevalier, Johnny Cash on a good day and Earl Long anytime. He was a natural."

No one, Chevalier believes, could politic any better. "Aside from his cussing, drinking, gambling and carousing, he was the best Christian I knew." And boy, could he work both sides of the fence. In Catholic Cajun country, he would hold up his graduation ring from Loyola University and say if it wasn't for the good Catholic professors, he would have never gotten a law degree.

In central and north Louisiana, he would rail on about how his mother was a rock-ribbed Baptist and how his Baptist grandparents drove to church in a horse-drawn buggy.

About seven years ago, Chevalier said, the London Times did a story on the seven most influential families in the United States. Listed among them were the Carnegies, the Roosevelts, the Rockefellers and the Longs of Louisiana.

"Russell Long was the most powerful man in the Senate for 25 years," he said. "Huey's gone, Earl's gone, the legacy is gone, and there's no one left with the mettle of those three men."

Chevalier talked about Andy Warhol's theory of everyone having 15 minutes of fame. "Everything is a moment in time. Blaze had her moment and it lasted a year and a half. I had my moment with Earl and it lasted 13 months. Now lightning might be striking again." At the recent Tennessee Williams Festival, in which Chevalier participated, he said he was the only author to run out of books to autograph and sell.

There's an old Nashville adage about songs, which Chevalier hopes applies to books: "You can't hype a dog and you can't stop a hit."

Sounds like vintage Uncle Earl.

The Gorilla Man Kept His Promise

May 28, 2003

When Rodney Fertel died last week, it opened a floodgate of memories back to the '60s and '70s when this city had a thriving colony of wonderfully hilarious eccentrics.

The ringmaster of these Runyonesque characters was clearly Allen "Black Cat" LaCombe, the legendary Fair Grounds handicapper and publicity director who once ran for governor in 1959. One of his gubernatorial banners said: "Run the squirrels out of office – keep the state safe for the nuts."

LaCombe, from a small town in Avoyelles Parish named Echo,

moved with his family to the Irish Channel as a child and became the epitome of the con artist characters that area of the city produced. He hung out with sportswriters and reporters, who he called "da news guys."

In LaCombe's stable, among others, were Leapin' Lou Messina, who promoted boxing events with the Black Cat, and Curley Gagliano, who owned Curley's Neutral Corner at St. Charles and Poydras, a sports bar for boxing fans, racetrackers and reporters. Some called it the home of the "write and fight crowd." It was there where LaCombe took the dare from his cronies to run for governor.

But Rodney "Get the Gorilla" Fertel, also part of Black Cat's entourage, may have topped 'em all. Fertel was the kind of guy that columnists live to write about. In 1969, the gambler and racetracker who had inherited a fortune ran for mayor. It was to be a campaign never before seen in this city — or anywhere else.

He pledged that if elected, he would get a gorilla for the Audubon Zoo. His campaign manager was none other than the Black Cat.

"Don't settle for a monkey," said the candidate. "Elect Fertel and get a gorilla. If elected, I will conduct a personal safari to the Belgian Congo at my own expense and bring back two live gorillas to the Audubon Zoo."

This may be difficult to believe, but it is true. I witnessed it. Fertel had 50,000 miniature gorillas made – 25,000 white and 25,000 black. That was so people knew he did not harbor any racial prejudice. He bought campaign buttons with King Kong's face on them.

Then he put on a gorilla costume and walked up and down Canal Street giving out his gorillas and buttons. Gorillas, he informed people, would get your mind off of such worrisome things as Vietnam and help you relax. LaCombe also got Fertel an invitation to appear before The Press Club of New Orleans where he made a speech wearing his gorilla suit.

If he wasn't in his gorilla outfit, he wore a pith helmet and carried binoculars, looking like some sort of safari wannabe. In the November election that year, of 176,736 votes cast in the

Democratic primary, the Gorilla Man got 310. So what did he do then?

In 1970, he went straight to Singapore, which even the geographically-impaired will tell you is nowhere near what was the Belgian Congo. He began his search for the gorillas. He would send letters to me and my colleague Gene Bourg at the old States-Item informing us of his progress.

Months went by. The letters kept coming. One day I got a picture of him riding around Singapore in a convertible wearing his gorilla outfit. He was giving the "thumbs up" sign. Fertel had scored.

But you know what? He kept his promise. Losing the election – and even a gambler such as Rodney would have set odds of 2,000-1 or higher – never deterred him from his mission. He bought two gorillas for the zoo. "Anybody can buy an elephant or a tiger," he told me, "just pick up the phone and go buy them. But try to get a gorilla."

Later on in the '70s, when the apes were firmly bedded down at the zoo, he purchased a television and put it in their cage so they could watch their favorite shows. He delighted in going to the zoo and sitting for hours watching and talking to them. He even named one of his racehorses Fertel's Gorilla.

I still have two miniature plastic gorillas – yes, one black and one white – and the King Kong campaign button. They are highly cherished possessions. As are the memories of Rodney Fertel and all those characters in the New Orleans Rogues Hall of Fame.

Diamond Jim Moran: A Shining Example

July 17, 2005

Diamond Jim Moran was the flamboyant impresario of La Louisiane restaurant who was famed for putting diamonds into his customers' meatballs and wearing head-to-toe diamonds and outrageous clothes on his annual treks to the Kentucky Derby.

Even before taking over the restaurant in 1954, he was one of this city's most colorful legends, rising from a shoeshine boy to a boxer to a barber who cut Huey Long's hair and later became his bodyguard and confidant. His friendship with Long, Mayor Bob Maestri and the gambling and racketeering underworld is credited with leading to illegal slot machines coming to Louisiana and his and his cronies' personal wealth.

Moran lived life in the fastest of fast lanes, hanging out with movers and shakers, celebs, politicians, judges, racetrackers, sports figures and the fight crowd. He was charming, could cook, had a voracious appetite and a penchant for booze.

He hobnobbed with the likes of Jimmy Durante, Rocky Marciano, Jack Dempsey, Liberace, Abbott and Costello and Johnny Carson, who all dined at La Louisiane.

Gov. Earl K. Long and stripper Blaze Starr of the Sho-Bar on Bourbon Street used his restaurant's third floor apartment for their rendezvous. Marciano once delivered a Cadillac to Moran with the words "Diamond Jim Moran: Food For Kings" on the side. This was Diamond Jim's world.

When Moran died of a heart attack with his diamonds on at his power table in his restaurant, nationally syndicated and controversial columnist Robert Ruark was on assignment in Spain. Ruark stopped what he was doing and wrote about Moran, who was born James Brocato, but changed his name so his mom wouldn't know he was boxing.

"Jimmy was – I suppose you could call him an ex-hoodlum in a mild sense," wrote Ruark, "since he was mixed up with the Frank Costello mob in the slot machine business, and did a little time in the clink, and had been a bootlegger. And I say the hell with it. Diamond Jimmy was, in his peculiar way, real class, and he dropped dead the other day, and he was working when he departed.

"Jimmy had diamonds in his teeth and diamonds on his fingers. One time he gave me a diamond-studded pump gun. One time I gave him a pair of leopard-skin spats and he wore them to the Kentucky Derby with tremendous success. Mostly what he gave me was a non-computable friendship. That's a commodity that's harder to come by than diamonds or leopard-skin spats."

La Louisiane began as a hotel and restaurant in 1881, at its current site on Iberville right off Bourbon Street. Originally operated by Louis and Anne Bezaudun, it later became one of the city's best under the guidance of Fernand Jules Alciatore, a famous name in the culinary history of the city.

But clearly its most colorful owner was Diamond Jim, who purchased the property in 1954. After his death at age 61, two of his sons, Tony Moran and Jimmy Moran Jr., continued operating the restaurant until 1978, but it was never quite the same without its star attraction.

Now, new co-proprietors Brett Smith and his mother, Jaye Berard Smith, have completed a grand historical renovation, retaining the integrity of the historic walls, original brickwork, natural cypress and gold-leaf ceilings — and taken it back to the days of Diamond Jim. Calling it La Louisiane Bistro & Bar, there are many photographic reminders of Diamond Jim's heyday.

And there are some touches that Diamond Jim would appreciate. Moran surrounded himself with good-looking women and many a picture was taken of him with a blonde drinking out of an ice bucket that held three beers and was a signature drink at La Louisiane.

Jaye Berard Smith, or "J.B.," as she is known, is an accomplished artist who has painted in oils over gold and silver leaf to depict beautiful women throughout the restaurant. The women are all friends of hers, and she painted them as she recalled them from years ago. One is even painted in the nude – on the men's room wall.

The women dine together in the restaurant from time to time. General Manager Eric Bay likes to tell the story of the customer who was told that the ladies in the paintings were there that day, dining, and were pointed out to him.

The man walked up to their table and said, "I just want to know which one of you is in the men's room."

"They all raised their hands," Bay said.

In the main dining room, there are four tables in the round, each in a corner, one of which is the "Power Table" at which Moran ate his last meal.

Bay and Brett Smith put out the word that they were looking for memorabilia and stories came pouring in. "I got more and more involved in the story," Bay said. For example, he learned that when famed women's golfer Babe Didrikson Zaharias came here to play in a tournament, Moran presented her with a diamond-studded ball marker.

Famed for his enormous wardrobe, shoes and walk-in closet, not to mention his matching white ermine sports coat, hat and tie, Moran was "50 years ahead of his time – pimp daddy bling." Bay said.

The Kentucky Derby was where Moran really shined. His annual arrival at the Louisville track – he made 30-plus trips in a private L&N railroad car — was a media event of enormous magnitude. Surrounded by his entourage and bodyguards and trailed by autograph hounds and the press corps, he easily outshone such guests as Bob Hope and Princess Grace of Monaco.

"I've got suits that would rival some of the Coronation robes in England," he said one year. "I'm so loaded with jewelry, pal, I don't know where I'm going to hang most of it." Somehow, he always managed.

Since Moran was involved with a speakeasy and served time in federal prison for violation of the Volstead Act, he would no doubt approve of the restaurant's first-floor restroom next to the bar. One-way mirrors allow the occupant to see through the walls around him.

"You can see out but they can't see in," Bay said. "You'll know if someone's messing with your date."

Also remaining is the famed door that led from the restaurant to the infamous Playboy Club, which was next door.

Much of the information Smith and Bay obtained about Moran came from one of his four sons, Dr. Bobby Brocato. A dentist who lives in Many, La., he is well-known for being a patron of the famed Joe W. Brown racing stable, which named one of its finest stakes horses after him, Bobby Brocato. He also made trips to the Derby with his dad.

Moran entertained the likes of Lucky Luciano, Frank Costello, Carlos Marcello and other "business associates" four or so times a year at his summer home on Lake Pontchartrain. He was eventually called to testify before the Committee on Crime and Racketeering headed by Sen. Estes Kefauver.

When Moran arrived, he was in full regalia: Adler's diamonds across the bridge of his eyeglasses, collar pin, stickpin, diamond-studded false teeth, cufflinks and rings; even his zipper sported diamonds. Bobby Brocato said his dad's attorney Monk Zelden flipped out when he saw how his client was adorned and suggested he remove the glitter.

Moran asked Monk if his testimony was going to be on national TV and Zelden said yes. "Well, the ice stays," Moran said.

Moran not only testified, but according to newspaper reports, "He answered all questions thrown at him, some of them hilariously. In the end, he invited Sen. Kefauver to go duck hunting with him."

Kefauver, one of the most dogged and tenacious Congressional investigators, not only wound up being one of Moran's friends, he wrote the eulogy for him in the Congressional Record when he died.

Actor Robert Taylor once said, "Barbara Stanwyck and I agree Diamond Jim could give sex appeal to an onion."

Can't say for sure about the onion, but the Smiths have clearly brought the sex appeal and ambiance of Diamond Jimmy's day back to La Louisiane

CHAPTER 3
Holidays

Father's Day:
If Only Dad Could Drop By Today

June 17, 1990

Earlier this week, when my kids asked me for a hint about what I wanted for Father's Day, I gave it to them. I'd like a baseball reference book I've had my eye on, and if I've behaved myself, the chances are good they and their mom might find it for me. But that's not the point.

The point is that what I really wanted to tell them is this: I've already got what I want most in life for this and every other Father's Day – a nice family. No man could be more blessed. But if I could ask for something else – it would be an impossible request – it would be this: I wish my dad could drop in for a day, see what I did with my life and take a look at his grandchildren.

Since 1977, when I started writing this column, I've written about a lot of personal things. It's not that what has happened in my life is so important, it's just that I learned a long time ago from other columnists, who had been at it longer than I have, that readers relate to what's going in your life simply because they may have had a similar experience.

It could be any subject, from something as ridiculous as the time I went looking for a stamp in my wife's purse and couldn't believe the stuff she had in there – so I emptied it out in disbelief, and wrote that her purse was better stocked than most convenience stores. Or it could be something as frustrating as picking a slow-moving line in a bank, then changing lines, only to see the line you left suddenly zoom forward.

It could be buying a car that turns out to be so big a lemon it's laughable, trying to assemble a dollhouse with 200 parts at 3 a.m. on Christmas morning, not being able to decide which kitten to adopt and coming home with two, or losing a dear friend. That's life, and sooner or later it happens to all of us.

I've tried to share some of these experiences in a timely fashion, so this week as I do every year around Father's Day, I thought a lot about my dad, who died of a heart attack when I was 16.

Any death of a parent before children reach adulthood, of course, is tragic. In my case the situation was compounded by a couple of things. My mother had been a virtual bedridden invalid since brain surgery when I was 11 left her incapable of functioning or thinking normally. My dad had picked up the slack and we had been best pals, inseparable sports fans who attended just about any sports event known to man.

So it was ironic – and it was something I had to deal with for a long time after his death – that our great relationship would end on an argument about using the family car. We had some words as he dropped me off for school in the morning; I slammed the car door loudly and stormed away in anger, never to see him alive again.

No doubt there are more than a few dads or moms who have argued with their teen-agers about using the car. And no doubt there are other people who have said something in a heated moment to a relative or friend for whom they truly cared, and then endured the cruel irony of having them die before they could apologize.

Believe me, it's something you think about for a long, long time.

My dad was an immigrant to this country, coming here from British Honduras, which today is known as Belize. He married a New Orleans woman and was very proud to become a citizen, very proud to have received a banking degree from Tulane University's night school, and was one of the most devoted Tulane fans that school has ever known – to the point that he sold tickets on Willow Street. The memory of standing in ticket booths before going into the stadium with him on countless gorgeous Saturday afternoons is something I cherish fondly.

He was very strict, not surprisingly for someone of British

ancestry and upbringing. He believed education to be the most important thing in life and demanded I bring home good grades. Let's just say most of the time I passed muster. He was an excellent tennis player, enjoyed contract bridge, drank only on holidays and special occasions, smoked too much, and fought stomach ulcers most of his life.

He was a banker at the National Bank of Commerce, the treasurer of St. Andrew's Episcopal Church for probably 30 years or more, and as a young man in the '20s cut a dashing figure. I still have a picture of him all decked out in a white linen suit and straw katy, his foot propped up on the running board of a big black sedan.

He led a life devoid of female companionship after my mom's operation, and more than one person has told me the only thing that kept him going in life was me.

By the end of the school day we argued, I had cooled down. I took the streetcar home and sat on our steps, as I did every day, waiting for him to pull into the driveway. Only this day my uncle walked up and put his hand on my shoulder.

Late in the afternoon, my dad apparently started feeling bad and walked over to his doctor's office in the Maison Blanche Building. He did not leave the waiting room alive.

It took a few years, but with age, fortunately, comes maturity and understanding. I finally realized that arguments between dads and sons over using the car are a fact of life and, more importantly, I didn't need to live with the guilt that this argument, this one moment, had caused his death.

Unfortunately, there is no real answer as to why two people with such a wonderful, caring relationship – a kid who loved his dad, and a dad, I'm certain, who loved his son – had to end things this way. If anything, it's made what I have today even more precious.

I guess the only answer is: That's life. And I thank you for letting me share mine with you today. Happy Father's Day.

"Ein prosit!" Meets The Chicken Dance

October 3, 2001

When Germans get together they have this word which expresses warmth, good feelings, and comradeship.

And lots of singing, dancing and drinking, not necessarily in that order.

That word is "gemuetlichkeit." Don't try to pronounce it. Don't dare run it through your spell check. You can't stop it. You can only seek to contain it.

There will be a lot of gemuetlichkeiting going on at the Deutsches Haus this Friday and Saturday and the next three weekends after that. That's because the German beer hall at 200 S. Galvez Street opens its doors to the public for Oktoberfest celebrations with authentic German food, "schnapps girls," colorful flags and banners and of course, oom-pah-pah bands playing the "Chicken Dance," polkas and waltzes.

There will also be lots of people shouting "Ein prosit!" Prosit is Latin, not German, and very loosely translated, "Ein prosit!" means "One drink!" It's a German toast that says, "May it benefit you." Or something like that, depending on who you ask.

"They do a lot of 'ein prosits' here, about every third song," said Deutsches Haus board member and treasurer Alden Hagardorn.

Germans began migrating to this area as far back as 1840. There were two areas of the city where Germans settled, according to Deutsches Haus historian Richard Kuntz. One was bounded by Elysian Fields, Claiborne and Esplanade. It was known to some as the German Triangle, to others as Little Saxony. There was also another area in the Irish Channel near St. Mary's Church.

There were many German societies formed. Memberships began dwindling in the 1920s, so the leadership of the societies united, pooled their assets, and in 1928 acquired a large building on Galvez two blocks from Canal Street.

It had been the Cumberland Telephone Company, which was

subsequently bought out by Southern Bell for its Galvez exchange. GA was the prefix for a four-numeral phone number.

Volkfest, a May celebration with the Deutsches Haus decorated with lots of flowers and palms, had nothing to do with Volkswagens. Rather, it was a celebration of spring planting. Volkfest died out after World War II; the advent of air conditioning was a factor leading to its demise.

And as late as the '70s, Oktoberfest was only one Saturday night in October. But no more. Now it's five weekends of family fun which began last weekend. Children are welcomed and are a considerable part of the folk dancing and festive costuming. Also, this Sunday at 1 p.m. the German Heritage Festival Association will present its 15th annual Oktoberfest parade with German-themed floats and mini-beer wagons. And schnapps girls.

Women wear German costumes called drindls, a word that has caused a comment that German is the "buy a vowel" language. Men wear those funny-looking leather shorts with suspenders known as leiderhosen and tyrolen hats with little feathers in them and lots of buttons pinned on. It's quite a sight.

"It takes a certain amount of courage to wear leiderhosen," said Keith Oldendorf, the head of the German Heritage Festival Association and first vice-president of Deutsches Haus. "That's why we have the largest selection of German beers you'll find anywhere."

The membership in Deutsches Haus, now about 340, is open. You don't have to be German, just interested in German culture. Or have an interest from singing to collecting steins, or parading and sampling liquid refreshments such as Warsteiner, Bitburger or Franziskaner. Or enjoying knackwurst, sauerbraten and pretzels.

"One thing we do is that when we know of any Germans coming to the area, we invite them over," said Oldendorf, "so they can speak the language and feel comfortable. Two German frigates came into the port and the men came over and had a good time."

Heinz Kloth is a member and originally from Bremen. "The one thing a German never drops is a beer," he said, beer in hand. "I'm a kraut. Not a sauerkraut. I'm a happy kraut."

Karl Heinz is introduced as "a real German from Hamburg."

"He's a Hamburger," says a friend.

"No, I'm a Hamburgian," corrects Heinz. There is a lot of good-natured teasing at this happy establishment.

Anna Netzhammer Whitley has been coming to the Deutsches Haus since 1928 when she was 10. Her grandmother was one of the first to buy stock in the building. The family had a bakery on Oak Street. You can find Anna tending bar. "I open my mouth when I shouldn't," she said.

"That's a German thing – opening your mouth when you shouldn't," said Hagardorn.

The singing societies, including the Saengerchor, practice upstairs in the Saenger Halle (singing hall) and there are other groups that make it their home. The Schlarafia is a poetic society founded in Prague. It makes fun of aristocracy and adopts noble names. The Crescent City Homebrewers also use it for their clubhouse.

The roots of Oktoberfest can be traced to the royal wedding of Crown Prince Ludwig I to Princess Therese on October 12, 1810, in Bavaria. The whole city of Munich was invited to attend the festivities on fields near the city gates. Horse races with the royal family in attendance closed the event and when it was decided to hold the horse races in subsequent years, it began the tradition of Oktoberfest.

The Germans in Germany are amused by the continuing popularity of the Chicken Dance in U.S. celebrations. "It went out with 'Do the Hucklebuck' over there," said Kuntz.

There is considerable history in the Deutsches Haus. There are photographs in the upstairs Saenger Halle showing that the National Saengerfest was held here in 1890 in a large old wooden building at Lee Circle and again in 1958 at the Municipal Auditorium. Sigmund Odenhimer, a Jewish German, was the first president of Deutsches Haus and an Audubon Park philanthropist for whom the sea lion pool is named.

In 1931, the first bowling alley in New Orleans was installed at Deutsches Haus. There were six lanes. It was called Kegel Halle (bowling alley).

"So what's why they call a bowler a kegler," said Hagardorn. "I always thought it was because they drank a keg of beer." The popularity of the alleys declined after World War II when bowling alleys sprung up all over. They were removed in 1987. (Trivia: Germans bowl with only nine pins.)

The bands supplying the music for the celebration are the Deutsches Haus Hofkapelle and Prost! "Professor" Adrian Juttner teaches the "Schnitzelbank," an amusing and popular song that pretty much defies explanation.

And on November 1, the Waldmoessigen Accordion Orchestra will make an appearance at the Deutsches Haus. Virtually all-accordion and all-female, it prompted Hagardorn to say, "You just can't hear an all-girl accordion orchestra every day."

One amusing feature about the Deutsches Haus is the men's room, which is listed on a website named Urinals.Net as one of the world's finest. The men's room is called the "Herren Closet."

"That's confusing during Oktoberfest," said Hagardorn. "If that's the Herren Closet, where's the Hissen Closet?"

A Special Thanksgiving

November 24, 2005

One of my favorite passages from one of my favorite books, "A Short History of New Orleans," begins this way:

"It was a harsh, forbidding place to build a city," wrote WDSU-TV's Peabody Award-winning Mel Leavitt in 1982.

"Years later, when fever and floods and hurricanes repeatedly threatened to destroy it, a northern engineer exclaimed: 'New Orleans was built in a place God never intended a city to be built . . . six feet below sea level in the middle of a swamp, squeezed between a giant river and a huge lake.'"

The French, historian Leavitt tells us, called it Le Flottant — The Floating Land. Others named it La Prairie Tremblante – The Shaking Prairie. And the English dubbed it the Wet Grave.

Incredible quantities of water, he tells us, were a double-edged sword. It was and is the source of this city's predicament but also its raison d'etre — the reason for its existence and the means of its salvation. That would be a reference to the mighty Mississippi, the Father of Waters, the most vital transportation link for this nation.

Leavitt and I kept in touch through the years before his death, swapping stories and sharing notes. In light of what has come to pass and with Thanksgiving drawing nigh, I thought about his haunting words as I drove past one of my favorite haunts, Le Bon Temps Roule on Magazine Street.

There a new flag is flying that says, "Don't Give Up the Ship."

As Leavitt reminds us in his classic work, the most enduring of all Creole French sayings is, "The more things change, the more they stay the same." Katrina has given us pause to reflect on that wisdom.

I've thought a lot about all those things and also about what I might say at the Thanksgiving table today, the day we traditionally give thanks for our many blessings. To say the least, this one will be different, memorable, a little sadder and undoubtedly emotional . . . for many of us.

This may be difficult or even impossible for some people to comprehend, but even after the hurricane one of the things I'm most grateful for – other than my family and friends – is something I had absolutely nothing to do with.

So . . . I'll take this moment to thank the Good Lord and my parents for blessing me with the opportunity to live my life in New Orleans and Louisiana.

My dad, a British Customs Officer, emigrated to this country in the 1920s from what was then a British Commonwealth named British Honduras in Central America. Its capital was Belize, now the name and capital of the independent country. No doubt he could have chosen any city in the U.S. – some of his brothers and sisters chose other destinations — but he chose this enchanting, quirky, stylishly decadent city and married a New Orleans native.

I'm also thankful to have married a Texas lady who adopted my city as her own. We raised our family here and I'm thankful that they feel as passionate about their city as we do. No parent could ask for more.

And to have been blessed with having one of the greatest jobs in the world – which gives me the opportunity to write about this city and state I so dearly love, it goes without saying how much that means to me.

I'm in a unique position, as is my newspaper, The Times-Picayune, which I've been a part of for 35 years. Never before has a newspaper staff faced the challenge of covering arguably the most significant story in this country's history, undoubtedly the most important and compelling story in the city and state since they came into existence.

But it's not only a challenge, it's a blessing – because those of us who truly understand it and love this architectural gem, this food-worshipping, cuisine-crazed, music-mad, party-loving settlement – want to see it put back together not only the right way, but better than it ever was, without its sleazy politics, dysfunctional public education system, crime problems and racial tensions.

Which is saying a lot. But for that opportunity and challenge, my colleagues and I are thankful.

A couple of months ago, I don't think I would have said this, but I'm also thankful that Mardi Gras, even an abbreviated version, is on the calendar for 2006. I think we could all use a little mass therapy and so I'm thankful that decision has been made.

Even with the devastation, we need to maintain that parade mentality, that laid-back state of mind and party mindset that separates us from everybody else and makes our city unique. For those few days next February, we need to get back in the street and do what we do best, before we resume rebuilding our homes, our cities and our lives.

And for that opportunity to rebuild we should all be thankful.

What I say now comes straight from my heart: Pass the oyster dressing. Just kidding. God bless you and your family — and remember to give thanks for the most memorable Thanksgiving you will ever have.

And may God bless New Orleans.

Oh, Christmas Tree!

December 6, 2000

The ceilings in my grandmother's house were at least 12 feet tall, maybe 14, and in either case probably looked like 20 through the eyes of an 8-year-old. But every Christmas there was an enormous tree that filled up that space from floor to ceiling and about a quarter of what she called her front parlor.

Putting up the tree — which always came from Reuter Seed Co. on Carrollton Avenue and was always a blue spruce and always had to pass serious muster — was a magnificent operation that took considerable time and patience to get the tree looking the way she wanted.

Most everyone has a childhood memory about Christmas and this is mine:

To begin with, the trunk had to be trimmed down in order to fit the ancient but sturdy metal stand that held it and was literally nailed to the floor.

That done, the tree then was allowed to "fall," as my grandmother described letting the branches unfold or unfurl or whatever it is that Christmas tree branches do. This could take 24 hours or longer, until she was pleased with its appearance.

Then would come the alignment stage. No tree in my grandmother's house ever leaned to the left or the right, never tilted to the front or the back, or was ever the least bit off kilter.

Trees in her house were dead plumb. A construction crew putting up a fence could line their fence posts up off her tree, so perfectly vertical was it. This could take minute adjustments for more than an hour, but when it was done, it was . . . plumb.

Then came the testing of the lights. Back then there were no wimpy, tiny, throwaway strands of lights as there are now. These were heavy-duty strands with thick wire and were what she referred to as "series lights." They were large and beautiful, as I recall, but there was one hitch: When one light went out, they all went out.

And the same was true for "bubble lights," which she had a lesser amount of.

So if you plugged in a string to test it, and it didn't come on, the challenge was to find that one (and ideally only one) bulb that was burned out. It's one thing to find and replace a burned-out light when a string of 24 or 36 lights is stretched out on the floor. But when the lights are on the tree and all the ornaments and garlands and tinsel are hung, and you notice that there is a string of lights out, to then go searching for that one defective bulb . . . well, you might as well go looking for a four-leaf clover in winter.

But it happened every year that I recall, at least once, and it took considerable patience and dexterity, and usually a couple of people to get the tree back up to its illumination standards. Even if it was the day before the tree was to come down near Twelfth Night, it was unheard of to say don't worry about it. It was always done.

Aunts and uncles and grandchildren all pitched in, in varying degrees of participation, to get the tree trimmed. Easily the most time-consuming and tedious part of decorating her tree was the final touch — the hanging of the tinsel, or what my grandma called "icicles." Tinsel is not nearly as popular today as it once was, no doubt in part because it took a lot of time and patience to hang it properly in order to make it worth doing.

Tinsel was glittering and came in a box which contained hundreds of thin strips or threads probably about 16 inches long. These strips did not only glitter; they also clung together. And my grandmother did not like clumps of tinsel hanging on her branches. She liked individual strands, carefully placed and spaced on each branch at exactly midpoint of each strand. You needed a good set of fingernails and a lot of perseverance to be a tinsel person.

I was not a good tinsel person. My cousins, both girls, were a little better than I was, but when we were alone with no adults around, we simply flung the tinsel at the tree, an act of blasphemy that would have had us sent to Christmas purgatory or wherever convicted tinsel flingers are punished. Luckily, we were never caught in the act, although no doubt my grandmother wondered about some highly unorthodox tinsel formations on her tree.

Was she a perfectionist when it came to her Christmas tree? Was she demanding of those who did the work? Maybe. A softer, kinder description would be a laborer of love – as in lots of labor but also lots of love – a grandmother's love for her grandchildren.

The tree was always in the same spot, surrounded by a wall, some French doors that led to the front porch through which it could be seen, and her ancient crank Victrola. When the tree was all done, another ritual would begin. Someone would replace the "scratchy old needle" on the phonograph arm with a new needle, then turn the crank, which would be the non-electric force that made the turntable go-'round.

A 78 RPM record, usually featuring Christmas favorites from the early '50s, such as Gene Autry singing "Rudolph the Red-Nosed Reindeer" or Bing Crosby crooning "White Christmas," was then placed on the turntable, and the music would begin.

At which point the egg nog would appear and one of the uncles would produce a bottle of bourbon and we would all sit around and stare at our handiwork. Someone inevitably would stare at the top of the tree and say, "Don't you think the star's a little crooked?"

But by then the ladders had been put away and the men were into the bourbon, and even my grandmother had plopped into a chair and let down her guard. Yeah, by her standards, maybe it was a little off dead solid perfect. But you know what – you could still navigate off it.

And someone would always say the same thing: "I think it's prettier than last year." And it was, year after year.

CHAPTER 4
The Music Makers

Pete and the Prez

June 18, 2004

As the nation last week watched the tears and emotions of six days of national mourning for former President Ronald Reagan, perhaps no observers were more focused on the tenacity and grace of former First Lady Nancy Reagan than Beverly and Pete Fountain.

Legendary New Orleans clarinetist Fountain played for Reagan on four different occasions: when he was governor of California, at the first Reagan inauguration and at two state dinners at the White House.

The Reagans and the Fountains were married roughly the same number of years, respectively, and talked about that when the couples were together. The Fountains have been married 53 years and the Reagans were married for 52.

"Beverly taped everything that was on TV last week," Fountain said this week over a cup of coffee. "It really ripped me up, watching her and watching those kids. To know Nancy – she is such a love.

"To be a part of their lives, to be able to look back and say that we were there, is pretty special."

Fountain's connection to the Reagans began when Reagan was governor of California. Fountain was playing at a private men's club named The Grove north of San Francisco and Reagan was a guest. The musician and his band had to get back to Los Angeles quickly to play at the Hollywood Bowl, so a ride was arranged for them on an oil company's private plane.

Also on board was the governor and dancer/actor George

Murphy, one of Reagan's friends. The plane revved its engines and began its takeoff. Suddenly, out of nowhere, another plane crossed its path.

"We were all talking, had no seat belts on. We stopped cold, the takeoff was aborted and we all ended up on the floor," Fountain said. "All of a sudden this head pops up and it was Ronald Reagan. He smiled and said, 'Take 2.' "

Reagan's masterful delivery of jokes and wonderfully-timed clever one-liners was apparent in many of the retrospective clips shown last week, triggering Fountain's memory of how he wound up at the inauguration celebration.

Nancy Reagan's dad was a big fan of Lawrence Welk. Fountain played with Welk for years, and they had played for President Dwight Eisenhower. Mrs. Reagan called Frank Sinatra to see if he knew Pete. Of course, he did. Sinatra called Fountain and said, 'Pete, would you mind playing for them at a state dinner?' "

"Mind? Would I mind?" He was floored. "When and where?" he replied. "Whatever. Tell me and I'll be there." And so it began. Fountain was a hit and got invited back for an encore.

At the second state dinner, Fountain sat directly across from the president.

"A very crazy thing," Fountain recalled. "I'm thinking, it's hard to break into this scene. Nobody was speaking. Then Reagan began.

"He said if anybody ever has any problems hearing, get a hearing aid. It's wonderful. You wouldn't believe what sounds you can hear."

At that point, Fountain – who has no shortage of one-liners himself – could not resist. He asked Reagan: "Mr. President, can you pick up the baseball game on that?"

"On a clear night I can," said Reagan.

"That broke up the table," said Fountain, "me and my goofy self. Then everybody started talking.

"And I'm sitting there thinking what the hell am I doing here, sitting across from the President of the United States – an old boy from Warren Easton, a kid from White Street."

Sitting there amid white linen, presidential china, more silverware and crystal than any place setting he'd ever seen, with Abraham Lincoln's portrait staring down at him from a wall, and the finest cuisine – that he could not eat, not before a performance.

When Nancy Reagan found out he couldn't eat before he played, she offered him a doggy bag to take home.

"At a state dinner you're really playing for two presidents, so I also played for the president of Argentina and the president of Mali. So did I get uptight? Oh yeah, then I did and also when I played for the pope. I guess you could say I get a tingling feeling. Sometimes I think, how in hell did you do that? Maybe one day I'll clam up and get stage fright."

Fountain also played at state dinners for former Presidents George Bush and Richard Nixon. In the receiving line for Nixon, Fountain had his greeting prepared. He planned to say, "Mr. President, all New Orleans sends its love."

As he approached, Nixon said, "Hi, Pete, I read your book. I really enjoyed it." Fountain was shocked. His brain was short-circuited by Nixon's flattery. "I couldn't get my lines out," he said.

The White House engagements have allowed him and his wife to rub elbows with such luminaries as now California Gov. Arnold Schwarzenegger, actress Gina Lollobrigida, golfer Lee Trevino, pro quarterback Doug Flutie, singer Vicki Carr, Washington Redskins running back John Riggins and novelist Tom Clancy.

Fountain recalled: "Clancy had just written his first novel, 'The Hunt For Red October,' and Beverly sat at the same table with him. Not knowing anything about the book, she asked Clancy, "Is it fiction?"

And Clancy replied: "Isn't everything?"

Fountain last saw Nancy Reagan about three years ago when he played in Palm Springs, California, at the birthday party of former Ambassador Walter Annenberg, billioniare philanthropist, creator of TV Guide and publisher of the Daily Racing Form.

"I asked her, 'How's The Man doing?' And she just said, 'He's . . . OK.' We took a picture together," Fountain said.

That picture and those of the other presidential gatherings are treasured by the Fountains.

The clarinetist will be 74 on July 3.and still plays regularly at Casino Magic in Bay St. Louis.

"It's amazing. What a life Beverly and I have had," he said. "People are lucky to get to one state dinner. We've been to four. It scares me sometimes to think of all I've done. We've just been blessed."

The Nooge and K-Doe: Legends in Their Own Minds

July 11, 2001

Louie Nugent was vacationing in Amelia Island, Florida, when he got the news that his favorite singer and kindred spirit had passed away.

The real estate agent and retired New Orleans fireman just might have been Ernie K-Doe's number one fan. They sure thought and behaved alike. Nugent, famed for his zany antics, mastery of the non sequitur, bizarre outfits, eccentricities and love of music, has been known to wear a T-shirt that says, "I am a legend in my own mind."

"Well, I am," the man known as "The Nooge" said, "and so was he. That is totally applicable to Ernie K-Doe."

The legendary singer of "Mother-in-Law" and countless other hits including "T'aint It the Truth" died Thursday at Charity Hospital at age 65. He had served as this year's king of the Krewe du Vieux parade with wife Antoinette as queen and her cousin Tee Eva Perry as grand duchess.

The word around parade time was that K-Doe's next venture might be KDOE, a radio station featuring All-K-Doe all the time.

The flamboyant, often-unpredictable entertainer was one of New Orleans' chief characters, known for "speechifying," one of his K-Doe-esque terminologies. He loved to hold court at his beloved Ernie K-Doe's Mother-in-Law Lounge on North Claiborne and talk about anything and everything, but mostly about Ernie K-Doe.

"To be in the K-Doe lounge, playing the original cuts on the jukebox and having K-Doe behind the bar in our midst, singing along or mouthing the words, was a big part of my life," said Nugent. "I never ceased to get enjoyment out of listening to him. There was always a new little phrase, a new word, and some new K-Doe philosophy."

Nugent taped many of K-Doe's free-flow shows when he was a DJ at WWOZ-FM. "They still tickle me," he said. "With the K-Doe self-indulgence, if you're in sync with that, there's nothing funnier in the world."

Nugent is the force behind the wacky Mandeville Free Thinkers Society. A couple of years ago, that august group boarded a bus armed with blaring K-Doe music north of the lake, then picked up the K-Does and made several pit stops before arriving at the Jazzfest. One of those stops was at the steps of Charity Hospital, one of K-Doe's favorite forums.

"He made a big speech to a big crowd, told everybody his history, talked about how the walls went to shakin' and the nurses went to screamin' when he was born. Talked about the 'Star-Spangled Banner' and 'Mother-in-Law' being the only two songs gonna last to the end of the earth 'because someone is always gonna get married.'" And presumably, the USA will still be around and that other song will still be played.

"He was the only real magnetism we had left in terms of characters," said Nugent. "We got Dr. John, sure, but Dr. John ain't gonna let the Mandeville Free Thinkers Society pick him up in a bus and drive around with a bunch of drunks. Ernie would and did."

K-Doe was more powerful than even he probably knew. In the parking lot while tailgating before a Tulane-LSU football game one year, Nugent played tapes of K-Doe philosophizing.

"What is that?" asked an inquisitive fan.

"That's the Emperor of the Universe speaking. We're getting fired up!" said The Nooge.

"Why would you want to hear him talk about himself?" Nugent was asked. He just shook his head. "Man, that's the whole show. You don't get it, do you? You're listening to the Emperor of the Universe, not to be confused with the Emperor of the World.

"He definitely knew the universe was bigger than the world," added Nugent.

When the Millennium year arrived, K-Doe referred to himself as "Ernie Y2K-Doe." He definitely had a sense of humor, too.

During Mike Ditka's first year as Saints Coach, the Free Thinkers picked up the K-Does on a bus and took them to a game. "He told me it was the first Saints game he'd ever been to," said Nugent. For the occasion, K-Doe was decked out in head-to-toe black and gold, including a gold crown and cape. "Totally trimmed," said Nugent.

As they were walking from the Hyatt Regency Hotel on the concourse leading to the Dome, there was Marva Wright doing a pre-game concert. K-Doe, without much urging, got up on the stage and did one, then two, then three numbers, "and it's like he won't get off the stage," said Nugent. "People had just been walkin' by, and now they see this guy wearing a crown all tricked out, doing his walk and now the people are goin' nowhere. They're backed up to the Hyatt. That is the power that Ernie K-Doe had."

At the game, Nugent sat in front of K-Doe. He looked over his shoulder and there was Ernie lecturing these three guys a couple of rows behind him. "You know what's wrong with the Saints? It's them runnin' backs. But there's a simple solution. You got to tell them running backs: Run where they ain't. Run where they ain't. The problem with these boys is they run where they is."

"Sheer genius," said Nugent.

When Nugent joined the Marine Corps in 1966, one of the things he took with him was his "New Orleans Home of the Blues" album, featuring various New Orleans artists. After boot camp, he got to play it. It brought him back home. "Irma's great," he remembered thinking, "but Ernie's music has a special hop, skip and jump to it. That ah-ah-ah-ah-te-ta-te-ta-ta stuff, and that voice, there was no one else like him."

"Mother-In-Law" was No. 1 on the charts in 1961 and as K-Doe predicted, has not only endured but remained extremely popular through the years.

Nugent, of course, saw K-Doe at this year's Jazzfest.

"Front row," he said matter-of-factly. "Him and his capes and plumes, he really knew how to put on a show. He was still very energetic. When Antoinette got him to quit drinking, between her and his music, that kept him alive."

But now, it's over. "It's the end of an era for me," The Nooge said. "Now you can't bring people to the K-Doe lounge. You can, of course, but it'll never be the same without the Emperor of the Universe in there." T'aint it the truth.

(Louie Nugent died in 2006. He was the son of Louie "Liver 'n' Onions" Nugent, a colleague of the legendary Allen "Black Cat" LaCombe. Antoinette K-Doe died on Mardi Gras day 2009.)

Play It Again, Phil

July 20, 2007

"Piano Man" Phil Melancon was remembering that his very first night playing the Bayou Bar at the Pontchartrain Hotel couldn't have been any wackier.

"It was the day I retired from teaching after 21 years in elementary classrooms," he recalled, talking about the beginning of his 14-year gig there that regularly draws a raucous local crowd. "Now I really deal with children – only nobody raises their hand to go to the bathroom."

Melancon got the job as a fill-in for the regular piano player who had hurt his foot. "I was driving there on Carrollton past old Pelican Stadium and I'm thinking, 'What am I going to play? 'Walking My Baby Back Home,' some old standards? I didn't know."

For whatever reason, the satirical songwriter decided to open with "You're Gonna Moan for Momus, We're Not Parading Our Krewe."

All five tables walked out, the bartender was annoyed, rang out his register and told Melancon maybe he ought to take a break – after one song. Lesson learned quickly: Out-of towners are not going to dial in to local Carnival humor.

Not long after that, who should pull up in a brown and tan Rolls Royce but Allen Toussaint. "He gets some champagne, the place starts filling up again and I'm thinking, should I play his songs? No, he knows them too well."

So Melancon decided to play some sweet songs and when he took a break, Toussaint came up to him.

"He offers me this big soft hand and tells me I have very sensitive songs. I was so excited that I started playing so enthusiastically that the manager offered me the job full time. That's how it began."

Fourteen years and a ton of memories later, the curtain is coming down, the party's over. Melancon will play Friday and Saturday nights at 9. The Pontchartrain Hotel will shutter its doors when the last soul stumbles out onto St. Charles Avenue after his show Saturday night as it begins what has been announced as a six-to-eight month multi-million dollar renovation.

The once opulent and elegant landmark, famed for fine dining in the Caribbean Room, "Mile-high Ice Cream Pie" and celebrity guests such as Carol Channing and Helen Hayes, has declined to the point where it is nothing more than faded glory. A recent guest commented that she thought she was staying in a historic hotel, but said it was more like prehistoric.

One of those celebrity guests who graced the Bayou Bar was Ethel Kennedy, widow of Robert F. Kennedy.

"Ethel Kennedy came in with Jimmy Walsh. She ordered an Amstel Light on the rocks, I'll never forget that. Then she says, 'Oh, Phil, I've heard so much about you,' and I'm thinking what am I going to play for her? Certainly not 'Abraham, Martin and John.'"

So the mischievous Melancon asks her, "Mrs. Kennedy, what do you want to hear?"

And out of left field came this reply: "Ooo wah, ooo wah, cool, cool kitty, talk about the boy from New York City."

Not your regular piano bar standard, but, Melancon said, "I hit it, baby."

Melancon's satirical songs about public figures and local icons wax and wane in popularity because they are timely. But for years one of the most requested was his "Anne Rice" song in which he lampooned the vampire queen of the occult. He would begin with that one, saying, "Welcome to the beautiful Pontchartrain Hotel and the Bayou Bar, one of the few pieces of Uptown real estate Anne Rice has not purchased yet."

The song was written right after she bought the de-consecrated Mother of Perpetual Help Chapel on Prytania Street:

What a lovely chapel, is it for sale?
We'll alter the altar, install a television,
Put an island in the kitchen
Just for chopping chicken.

He recalled that there was a table of four women, one of whom was not amused. Turns out she was Rice's editor. "When I walked out that night, there used to be a picture of me on the wall. Well, it had a needle stuck in my nose. Did she do it? I don't know."

Melancon will quickly tell you that the audience picks up when his rotund sidekick Alden "The King" Hagardorn is in the house.

"When Alden's in the room, the room explodes — he's the most requested number," he said. Melancon and his showboating pal team up on several songs, including "Life is a Cabaret." And The Philettes, a group of singing female groupies, always seem to be on hand for big occasions.

Melancon stayed in the city for the storm. After Katrina, he entertained National Guardsmen. A couple of his most popular post-storm numbers were "Lootin' in the Morning', Lootin' in the Evenin', Lootin' at Suppertime" and "Old Aroma," to the tune of "Oklahoma."

Other standards through the years have been "I Wanna Job Just Like Arthur Hardy" and "On the Avenue." But he handles Nat King Cole standards such as "Unforgettable" and "Mona Lisa" flawlessly.

"By the time I walk into the place and I'm wearing my pink suit, I think I am Nat King Cole," he said. "I'm transformed."

What the Bayou Bar has provided is the perfect venue for a

cabaret piano player. Its configuration, its intimacy are ideal.

"You don't know how special it is until you start looking around at other places," he said. "Then there's that beautiful mural on the wall, the swamp scene. The boats start moving around one in the morning.

"In the best of worlds, they would renovate the hotel and invite me back, but I certainly have no hard feelings against the Pontchartrain. It's been a great run," he said.

But Saturday night promises to be very special, both Melancon and Hagardorn vow.

"Cole Porter sat at that piano, so did Armand Hug and Tuts Washington – he taught Professor Longhair to play," Melancon said.

Ironically, the last night Melancon will sit at the keyboard is his 55th birthday.

"What a wonderful birthday this is going to be," he said.

Why I Love Traditional Jazz

November 1, 2006

Trumpeter Mark Braud was a guest on Bob French's traditional jazz show on WWOZ last week, telling him about his new gig on Thursday and Friday nights at Snooks, the open-air bar at the corner of Bourbon and Orleans in the Bourbon Orleans Hotel.

When French heard that Braud's New Orleans Jazz Giants were playing from 7 p.m. to 10 p.m., he was surprised, commenting that jazz really doesn't get started until 10.

"They'll figure it out," he said.

Trad jazz in that time slot really appeals to a guy like me who has morphed from a late-night carouser who never watched the clock into an early-morning riser who enjoys seeing the sun come up after I get out of bed, not before I crawl into it.

While some say jazz gets better later at night – the old "the more

you drink the better we sound" adage — it's difficult to imagine finer versions of "Darktown Strutters Ball," "St. Louis Blues" or "Tiger Rag," with Freddy Lonzo's featured trombone providing the roaring riffs after "Hold that Tiger!"

Real, live street-corner jazz from old-line musicians who learned from their relatives playing on Bourbon Street – isn't this the way it used to be before T-shirt shops, loud canned rock music, daiquiri-to-go outlets, sleazy strip joints and guys carrying signs that say "Huge Ass Beers"?

Braud's jazz bloodlines are pure. He's 33, the grandson of the great trumpeter John "Picket" Brunious Sr., the nephew of internationally-acclaimed trumpeters Wendell Brunious and John Brunious Jr., and he attended the New Orleans Center for Creative Arts.

The crowd inside Snooks, which was named for legendary blind blues guitar great Snooks Eaglin, gets into it early, digging the talents not only of Braud but also his supporting cast, which includes drummer Ernie Ellie; sax and clarinet player Louis Ford; the engaging trombonist Lonzo; bassist Mark Brooks; and his brother, guitaritst Detroit Brooks.

"Is he really from Detroit?" a listener asks. "Maybe his mother liked Detroit."

No, he's as New Orleans as can be. And it's discovered later that he was named for his mother's uncle named "Detroy." The name's as good as it gets for a musician, but one from New Orleans? Brooks just calls it "a mistake." But a good one.

As the night wears on, the crowd moves in and out. People walking on Bourbon stop, stick their heads in the doorways, listen to a song or two and move on. Midway through the night, a familiar face walks in wearing his trademark bandana underneath his hat.

Kermit Ruffins sits down at a table with a couple of Bud Lights and joins the crowd's appreciation of the sounds, clapping to the music. "We have Mr. Kermit Ruffins in the house, y'all," says Braud.

A while later, at Braud's prompting — "Whatcha say, Kermit, come up and do one!" — Ruffins takes the mike, says, "Happy Thursday, y'all," and sings Frank Sinatra's "I've Got the World on a String," then rejoins the crowd to much applause.

"You're only as good as the band," he said, saluting the musicians.

"I rarely run into Kermit on Bourbon Street" Braud said. "Kermit found out this was happening and came on down. Thank you, Kermit."

The crowd voices its approval, as the musicians, all wearing black shirts and trousers, perform featured solos. When it's drummer Ernie Ellie's turn, he decides after a few hits on his drums and cowbell, that it's time to broaden his horizons.

So he gets up and plays his chair, then his microphone stand. Before you know it, he's drumming on the marble table tops, chairs, ashtrays, Kermit Ruffins's beer bottles, the bar, anything he can get his drumsticks on, short of the Swedish waitress bringing drinks around. Ellie is having a blast, enjoying his moment, the crowd is howling and clapping . . .

And I'm thinking, okay, you're supposed to be good at words – how I explain this to anyone who isn't from here? How do I explain why I just pulled the napkin out from under the chips in a basket we had ordered and started waving it over my head?

No need to explain this to Ruffins, who gives us a thumbs-up. No one else has done this with their napkins, but Ruffins and the band have picked up on it – that my wife and I are locals. That's what locals do. They second-line, even sitting at a table.

Why? Because. That's why. No explanation needed.

I keep thinking all night long about Bob French's mantra to his listeners: "Get out and hear some live local music!" We all should. We need to support these guys, we need them, they need us.

After one set, Freddy Lonzo, who started playing when he was 13, joins us and we start sharing, as Orleanians do, hurricane stories. Lonzo lost his home in Gentilly, may or may not rebuild and is living in Treme right now. And most of the guys in the band lost their homes. We ask how his gigs are going.

"October's been good. I don't know what the next month's going to bring, but September was a zero, a total zero," he said. Seemingly upbeat, he jokes about the future: "If you're a musician and you can't pay it off in one week, don't buy it."

"This is dedicated to all the ladies from all the men," says Braud, as the band swings into "Ain't She Sweet?" Then they kick it up a notch with Paul Barbarin's "Bourbon Street Parade," and well, even I know the words to this one:

Let's fly down, or drive down, to New Or-leeenz.
That city, has pret-ty, his-tor-ic scenes.
I'll take you, I'll pa-rade you, down Bour-bon Street.
There's a lot of hot spots,
You'll see lots of big shots,
Down on Bour-bon Street.

The finale is predictable. Braud calls it "the most requested song in New Orleans."

Oh when the Saints,
Oh when the Saints,
Oh when the Saints go marching in,
Lord how I want to be in that number
When the Saints go marching in."

I think I was. That's what my body said the next day.

How Ya Gonna Clap?

April 25, 2007

"What are you looking for?" my wife asked as I rummaged through a large closet.

"You know what I'm looking for," I replied.

"How would I know that?" she said. "I'm not clairvoyant."

"What time of the year is it? What's going on this week?" I said, tossing out a couple of clues. "You wanna buy a vowel?"

"The feedbags – you're looking for the feedbags for Jazzfest, aren't you?" she said.

"Correctamundo. I knew you were a bright woman."

When it comes to the Jazzfest, there are rituals and there are traditions.

Everybody has 'em, and I'm no exception. It's just part of getting pumped up for what's in store for the next two weekends and I can honestly tell you that as long as they've been around, I've always had a feed bag at the Jazzfest.

For the unenlightened or Jazzfest first-timers, a "feedbag" is a beer holder – some folks call 'em a huggie, others a koozie or coozie — only the feedbag has a roughly 24-inch cord running through it that allows you to hang it around your neck, freeing up your hands.

"How ya gonna clap?" is the motto that's been on the side of these ingenious devices for years. And that's practical advice too; you don't want to dump your beer on someone in front of you while you're clapping for a performer.

Every once in a while you see a different slogan on them, such as the year when this message appeared:

"Party like an animal: Strap on a feedbag."

Simple enough directions. Just lead me to the trough.

I'm embarrassed to tell you how many of these things I have. But while I always take an old one out on the first day of the fest, just in case – heaven forbid! – that they are not available, I usually buy one or two or even more each year.

Like baseball caps and T-shirts, you can't have enough feed bags, I always say – which is not what my wife says.

The feedbags work amazingly well on parade routes, too. They are very colorful: Shocking pinks and greens and yellows seem to be the norm for the all-important cord. The feedbags themselves, well, you know what – I'm looking at about 30 of these things and there really isn't any consistency.

Sort of like my life.

I can still recall the very first time I saw them being hawked by vendors on Fortin Street, right outside the Fair Grounds at Jazzfest time. I bought one and thought, "This is sheer genius." It was a very special moment – I really bonded with that feedbag and it's been that way ever since. I can't imagine Jazzfest without one.

I mean, invention-wise, you'd have to rank it up there with, well, certainly not the Internet, because Al Gore invented that.

Nor is it in a class with elevators, air conditioning,

Barcaloungers or GPS. But surely it's on a par with fly swatters, Frisbees, pogo sticks, Rabbit corkscrews, Yo-Yos, Tupperware, toilet landing lights and diaper alarms – all noble, practical contrivances and conveniences.

This year I may go with the tenth anniversary "Festival Feedbag" edition, which celebrated a decade of "How Ya Gonna Clap?" Or maybe I'll just take 'em all and decide when I park.

Besides the obvious – collapsible arm chairs and a hat or cap — there's another piece of equipment that always goes with me to the fest. It's my WWOZ backpack/drink cooler that has handy zippered pockets for Jazzfest maps, sunblock, handy wipes, my wife's lipstick, and . . . extra feedbags for friends.

Now that I'm revving up the full festival mode engines, I'm already visualizing where I'm going to establish my beachhead, my center of operations on Friday. This is my command post, where I pitch my chairs and gear and where I would give commands if only there were someone who would listen to them.

This is where my group regroups between acts, where I finalize the day's game plan, where I chill and where I graze, which is perfect if you're named Angus.

And it's always the same spot: Way, way in the back of the Acura stage – it's actually on the Fair Grounds turf course — where it's not so claustrophobic, where there's more air on a hot day and it's near the Fair Grounds' dirt course, which gives you quick access to the bank of portable potties.

There is also usually a refreshment stand nearby, so you've got the two most important pieces of the puzzle solved – comfort and thirst.

Everything else is a bonus: the food, the music, the sights. You know what I tell people? You can't miss. Cochon de lait po-boys, crawfish sacks and mango freezes meet Eddie Bo and Dr. John. If you can't have fun at Jazzfest, face it: You can't have fun.

And as the day wears on and inhibitions are slain, it's the best people-watching scene this side of Mardi Gras day in the French Quarter. For booty shaking, it can't be beat.

And what's so bad about that?

Two of a Kind: Pete Fountain and Tim Laughlin

April 25, 2009

Watching and listening to Pete Fountain and Tim Laughlin play their clarinets together is sheer magic. Two wizards waving melodic wands that produce some of the most remarkable sounds you'll ever hear – and having the time of their lives doing it.

"Pete and I just enjoy listening to each other. We kind of lean on each other. It's so great to stand next to a legend," said Laughlin, who wrote a song named for his idol – "For Pete's Sake" – on his new CD, "A Royal St. Serenade."

Laughlin will join Fountain during the latter's performance at the People's Health Economy Hall Tent today. They warmed up by performing together last Friday at the French Quarter Fest, Fountain's first gig since a recent hospitalization.

"It's always special being with Pete and it was kind of a home-coming for him," Laughlin said. "A lot of people hadn't seen him in a while, so they wanted to see how he's doing. He played really strong. He sounded good."

These are two charismatic fun-loving New Orleans musicians: one 46, one 78; one who has been to the top of his mountain, having played for presidents and a pope, the other undoubtedly destined for it. It's a mutual admiration society that comes across every time they're on stage together – along with their love for their hometown, New Orleans.

A lot of people make comparisons between their lives. They began playing at the same age, 9. They both had incredible instructors and similar influences, including Benny Goodman. They both play New Orleans-style jazz, blues and swing. They both wear their emotions for their city on their sleeves. One's bald, the other's balding. And they're both redheads.

"Pete, I'm going to have to take your word on that," said Laughlin, who is still red.

Laughlin met Fountain at age 17 and has walked with Pete's

Half-Fast Walking Club on Mardi Gras day ever since. He plays a clarinet that Fountain gave to him, which he cherishes.

"It's the same clarinet he used when he was on Lawrence Welk's show, the one he made his first 10 albums with," he said. It's nicknamed "Old Betsy."

"Tim is a great player, in my opinion the greatest clarinet player in the country now, and that includes everybody, even me," said Fountain, who played with Connie Jones and the French Quarter Festival All-Stars at the recent French Quarter Festival. After he played his signature song, "Just a Closer Walk With Thee," he retired from the stage to a thunderous ovation from many misty-eyed onlookers.

"I see now that he means as much to you as he does to us," Jones told the audience. "Thanks for showing him such respect. He's a legend."

"Through the years you don't get those kind of ovations much," Fountain said. "I enjoyed that. It's a good feeling to be with guys you enjoy." Not to mention the crowd, many of whom tried to tell him hello after he left the stage.

"Jazz is just a communication between musicians. It's kinda like having dinner with an Italian family – everybody's talking at once, having a good time," Laughlin said of the jazz ensemble that day. "It's like organized chaos. You get the right musicians together and it's magic. The people see that and join in the fun. The biggest kick is that you're part of a unit and nobody's sticking out.

"That's the essence of what separates New Orleans jazz from Chicago jazz – everything's about dance, making people move. And Pete has the amazing ability to do that."

Laughlin and his group will play the Economy Hall Tent on Friday. The playlist will no doubt include the song he wrote for Fountain, which starts out bluesy, gets more complicated and quirky, sort of like you don't know what to expect.

"I try to look at the personality of the person I'm writing for," Laughlin explained. "The thing I like about Pete is his humor. He's just one of those guys who make you laugh. And you never know when it's coming."

There's another original song on the CD, a beautiful tune named "A Song For Juliet." Laughlin was playing a gig on the steamboat Natchez in 2006 and met a woman named Juliet Kim. She had come to New Orleans, her interest piqued by a college course she took that involved the history of New Orleans. He invited her over for tea the next day. They hit it off, and they kept in touch after she went home to Orange Beach, Calif.

Last October she was in town. Her birthday is Oct. 12 and that night Laughlin was playing a gig at the Napoleon House and she had another party to go to. She came by before he started playing.

"I wanted to surprise her," he said. He played the song, then told her, "I have something for you. Happy Birthday. This is something to remember the rest of your life." He gave her a CD with the song on it.

They were married in December at their home on Royal Street. Connie Jones and Pete Fountain were there.

"I think there was a strong connection between New Orleans, my music and the love I have for the city," he said. "She's become a big advocate for New Orleans."

So "A Royal St. Serenade," the CD with a song for his new wife and a song for Pete, is obviously special.

"It felt good, that's the most important thing," he said. "And if it feels good, you've done your job."

The Star-Spangled Banner: Sing It Irma's Way

August 15, 2001

When raspy-voiced singer Macy Gray sang an offbeat version of the National Anthem and fumbled the words in her hometown of Canton, Ohio, at the recent Pro Football Hall of Fame game, she got booed — and joined a growing list of name singers who have done a number on "The Star-Spangled Banner."

"I didn't see it but that's really bad if she got booed. She just didn't do her homework," said New Orleans Queen of Soul Irma Thomas. "I must have sung that song a thousand times or more and I've never had a problem with it."

Some singers, like Gray, like Jose Feliciano, like Aretha Franklin, just felt they had to do their own interpretation. And they bombed. "It did happen to Aretha. She was so busy trying to Aretha Franklin-it-up, she forgot the words," said Irma.

"You just don't jazz it up," she said. "You keep it simple. It wasn't written to be jazzed up. If it ain't broke, don't fix it. When I sing it, it's just Irma singing the National Anthem. I've always been comfortable with it. I respect the song."

That got me to thinking about the best and worst National Anthems I've ever heard.

As we approach a time in the sports year when baseball and football overlap, if you are a sports fan, rest assured you will be hearing more different versions than you ever hoped for of Francis Scott Key's inspirational tune written during the shelling of Baltimore's Fort McHenry in the War of 1812..

We all know about the bad efforts. In 1990 at a San Diego Padres game, one of my not-so-favorite people, Roseanne Barr, not only sang off-key and screamed the lyrics so they were unintelligible, she also grabbed her crotch, apparently pretending to imitate a baseball player. Not-so-funny Roseanne bombed out bigtime. President George Bush called it "disgusting."

Robert Goulet's miscue might not have ever been noticed had it not been at one of the biggest sporting events of the 1960s, the rematch of heavyweight champion Cassius Clay (now Muhammad Ali) and Sonny Liston in Lewiston, Maine, in May of 1965. If memory serves, Goulet lost track right at the beginning when he sang, "Oh say can you see, by the dawn's early night . . . "

In fairness to Goulet, he had lived in Canada since he was a teen-ager and had never sung the anthem in public before, but the mistake still haunts him.

If you've ever listened to fans around you singing along, no telling how many times the words "fight" and "night" have been swapped around – as in "through the perilous fight" which has been "through the perilous night" on many occasions. Similarly, "gave proof through the night that our flag was still there" has turned into "gave proof through the fight that our flag was still there."

Contributing to the confusion is the fact that if you swap the words, the lines still make sense. And in addition to "night" and "fight," the words "light," "bright" and "twilight" are also in the song, enhancing the potential for slips of the tongue.

Feliciano was the guy who started the interpretative renditions of the National Anthem back in 1968, for better or worse. When Dr. John sang his interpretation of the anthem before the Saints playoff game against the Rams last year, you could hear the crowd rumbling. They love Dr. John, he's the man, but this is The Star-Spangled Banner and we don't need to hear this gritty voice singing a funky bluesy version of it. Talk about "Right Place, Wrong Time," that was it.

"Dr. John's not a singer, he's Dr. John – he'll tell you that himself," said Irma. "He's out of his league with that song. If you don't know what you're doing, it'll eat you up."

Thomas prefers to sing it a cappella. "If you find the right key, it's really not tough," she said. And even though she's done it over and over again, when she's heading to an event to sing it, she'll practice it a couple of times in the car.

Everybody from Garth Brooks to Aaron Neville has sung the National Anthem but the very best version in my opinion had nothing to do with singing. Saxophonist Gary Brown of the 544 Club on Bourbon Street played it solo at a Tulane football game a few years ago and it was fabulous. Brown was hired to do every Arena football game here and more than one person said he was better than the games.

Al Hirt, when he was right, did a good job, too.

True, there are words to the song, so when it's an instrumental, you're counting on the crowd to sing the words, and that rarely happens. But the instrumental touch works for me.

Thomas' favorite is a rendition by Marvin Gaye. "It was at a basketball game and it brought tears to your eyes with that great voice and his smooth easygoing manner."

What the sports fans of America don't need is a tricked-up version of the National Anthem. And we don't need some cute little 5-year-old whose parents think he can sing shattering our eardrums with an off-key version that seems to last forever.

My feeling is this: Keep it simple. Keep it upbeat. Don't drag it out. It's a patriotic song sung to the tune of an old British drinking song. It's not a love ballad. It doesn't have to last five minutes. It doesn't need interpreting. The fans are ready to rock and roll. They don't need a downer. They need an upper, a spirit-lifting version that keeps the joint jumping.

The Chicago Cubs have guest singers but when they don't they use public address announcer Wayne Messmer, who is as steady and dependable as they come. Nothing fancy, just sung the way it ought to be before a ball game.

He's not Whitney Houston, but he gets the job done. Like Irma said, "If it ain't broke, don't fix it."

CHAPTER 5

This Is a Vacation?

Up on Cripple Creek

September 2, 1985

About two weeks ago I was getting off a narrow-gauge railroad train in Cripple Creek, Colo., and stopped to thank the engineer, Curtis Fox, for his guided tour of what was once the site of the nation's richest gold mines. I asked him how Cripple Creek got its name.

"Well," he said, "there was this cowboy named Levi Weldy, they tell me, and one day his saddle horse broke his leg in the creek. Then, the next thing you know, a couple of his calves broke their legs in the creek. Then when his son broke his leg in the creek, I guess he decided it wasn't much good of a creek, and said enough is enough. So he named it Cripple Creek."

It may not have been much of a creek, but it was one hell of a gold mine. From 1890, when gold first was discovered, until 1961, when the last mine shut down, more than $500 million worth of gold ore was dug out of Cripple Creek. I also learned that from Curtis, the fact-filled engineer.

As my family and I walked down the stairs of the railroad station I turned to my wife and said, "Boy, that was interesting. I always wanted to know how it was named, didn't you?"

"I guess so," she said.

"Did you know that the first newspaper in Cripple Creek was named The Crusher?"

"No, I didn't," she said.

"Well, it was. I think it's the little details that make a vacation so memorable, don't you?"

"Whatever you say, dear. The kids want to get some lunch. Is that OK with you?"

"Don't you want to see the Palace Hotel, where the stagecoaches unloaded?"

"I think they're hungry," she said.

We settled in at the Hungry Miner café, ordered a buffalo burger, and over lunch I got to thinking that vacationing with me is a little bit like vacationing with Chevy Chase. I kinda enjoy driving all over the back roads in search of the world's third largest freestanding mud house, or the world's largest ball of twine, or the largest artichoke ever known to man.

One gold town wasn't enough for me, either. No sir. Not only did I drag us to Cripple Creek, which is southwest of Colorado Springs, but I took us more than a hundred miles in the other direction so we could check out Central City, which is west of Denver. Now, Central City is no Cripple Creek, admittedly, but how often do you get a chance to stop in the bar where Buffalo Bill drank his whiskeys?

That's correct. On the wall of the Toll Gate Saloon in Central City was a sign that read, "Buffalo Bill Drank Here."

"Is that true?" I asked the bouncer wearing a Colt .45. "That's what the sign says, Slick," he replied. "You guys hear that? Buffalo Bill drank here!" I said.

"Who was Buffalo Bill?" my daughter asked.

"Sure, Dad," said my son. "He drank here – right across the street from the Bonanza souvenir shop."

"Never mind," I said. "We're here, and we're going in."

"You think that was here when Buffalo Bill was?" my son asked, pointing to a large mounted bison head with a sombrero hanging on one of its horns. "Let's just enjoy a little history," I said. The waiter came around for our order. "Four sarsaparillas," I said.

"What's that?" asked my daughter.

"That's what you order when you come in a place like this," I replied.

The band on stage began to warm up and I spotted a sign which read, "Vaudeville's dead – and we may have the acts that killed it."

"If Buffalo Bill drank here," my wife said, "he was some kind of weirdo. It says here in the walking book tour that this used to be a funeral parlor."

After admonishing my group that they had absolutely no respect for folklore, I took us to the Teller House Bar, to see the legendary "Face Upon the Barroom Floor." That is the town's biggest claim to fame, the mysterious face in the story about an artist's ill-fated love for a woman "with eyes that petrified my brain, and sunk into my heart."

Everyone was truly impressed with the artistry and mystique, I should report, and there was nary a snicker to be heard. That is, until we pulled into Cripple Creek a couple of days later and wandered into a bar famous for – its mysterious face on the floor.

Oh, well. There was a lot of time left, so I made sure we went to see the legendary kissing camels at the Garden of the Gods. No trip to Colorado is complete unless you see the kissing camels, which really aren't camels, of course, but large rock formations that do look like what you would expect camels would look like kissing. "Is that something, or what?" I asked my wife.

"That's something," she replied.

"Wait till we drive to the top of Pike's Peak this afternoon," I said.

(Angus Lind and Chevy Chase share a birthday in October. They are both well-balanced Libras.)

A Crazy Sight on the Ski Slopes

January 11, 1988

If you've never been skiing, you might not appreciate this story. But give it a try.

As a connoisseur of strange happenings and a skier, I can assure you that some of the strangest happenings anywhere happen on ski runs. But first, a word about those who dare to assault a snowy mountain.

Generally, those who go skiing fall into two categories:

Those who never return, whose biggest thrill is finally catching their breath, taking off their ski boots and jumping into a hot tub. There, they come to their senses and realize that no one should try a sport where there are ambulances and rescue units parked at the finish.

The second category falls in love with the sport. They block out all the negatives, the torture of putting on long johns, sweaters, parkas, caps, masks, goggles and heavy boots that immobilize your feet so you feel as though they've been sunk in concrete. They overlook the financial burden, the necessity of taking out a second mortgage to buy a three-day lift ticket.

They ignore the hassles, such as standing in a lift line for more than an hour for a 90-second run. All they tune in to is the orgasmic-like rush that skiing on a slope named Immediate Death provides for them. They spend the rest of their lives searching for more challenging mogul-laden black slopes to conquer. For this crowd, skiing's better than sex.

A friend just got back from a holiday ski trip to Utah with the kind of story that warms the cockles of anybody's heart. Conditions were perfect: 12 below, no feeling in the toes, basic numbness all over, the "tell me when we're having fun" kind of day. On the way up the lift there was so much griping that a rule was made that each person could complain for only one minute – then you couldn't bitch anymore that day.

One of the women in the group complained to her husband that she was in dire need of a restroom. He told her not to worry, that he was sure there was relief waiting at the top of the lift in the form of a powder room for female skiers in distress. He was wrong, of course, and the pain did not go away.

If you've ever had nature hit its panic button in you, then you know that a temperature of 12 below zero doesn't help matters. So with time running out, the woman weighed her options: She could relieve herself in her pants, or continue suffering. That was about it for options.

Her husband, picking up on the intensity of her pain, suggested that since she was wearing an all-white ski outfit she should go off in the woods, pull her pants down and relieve herself. No one would even notice, he assured her. The white will provide more than adequate camouflage. When you're desperate, any plan, even a bad one, sounds better than no plan. So she headed for the tree line.

There she dropped her ski poles, began disrobing and proceeded to do her thing. Now if you've ever parked on the side of a slope, then you know there is a right way and a wrong way to set your skis so you don't move. Yep, you got it – she had them positioned the wrong way.

Steep slopes are not forgiving, even during embarrassing moments. Without warning, the woman found herself skiing backwards, out of control, racing through the trees, somehow missing all of them, her derriere and the reverse side still bare, her pants down around her knees, picking up speed all the while.

She continued on backwards, totally out of control, creating an unusual vista for the other skiers. Her husband, realizing what happened, had long since gone to her rescue. Unfortunately, he was not as lucky as his spouse at dodging trees.

The woman skied – if you define that verb loosely – back under the lift, and finally collided with a pylon. The good news was that she was still alive. The bad news was that she broke her arm and was unable to pull up her pants. At long last, her husband arrived, put an end to the nudie show, then went to the base of the mountain and summoned the ski patrol, who transported her to a hospital.

In the emergency room, she was regrouping when a man with an obviously broken leg was put in the bed next to hers.

"So how'd you break your leg?" the woman asked, making small talk.

"It was the damndest thing you ever saw," he said. "I was riding up the ski lift, and suddenly I couldn't believe my eyes. There was this crazy woman skiing backward out of control down the mountain with her bare bottom hanging out of her clothes and her pants down around her knees.

"I leaned over to get a better look and I guess I didn't realize how far I'd moved. I fell out of the lift.

"So how'd you break your arm?"

East Side, West Side, All Around the Town

August 24, 2003

No good deed goes unpunished, a wise man once said. An Uptown couple couldn't agree more.

Richard Roussel months ago announced to his surprised wife Linda that he had planned a trip to New York – one of their favorite vacation spots — to celebrate her birthday. He had every detail covered and was very excited about it. They had a room at The Plaza Hotel. He ordered flowers in their room to surprise her when they arrived, and made three reservations at fine restaurants.

When they were about to depart, they ran into friends Bonnie and Peter Waters at the airport, who told them they were going to a resort near Atlanta. "Not us. We're going to the hustle and bustle and traffic of New York City and we can't wait," said birthday girl Linda. "We wish we were there right now."

Another wise man said, "Watch out what you wish for. It might come true."

To speed their arrival along, Richard decided they weren't going to check any bags.

They arrived in clear skies and the landing was perfect. It was 4:10 p.m. After a delay for the Jetway to arrive, the pilot came on with one disturbing announcement, then another and another. They say timing is everything. The Roussels had landed just as the blackout hit the Big Apple Thursday, August 14.

After an hour wait, the Jetway was manually moved to within about three to four feet of the plane. The passengers, with assistance from the crew, had to jump from the plane across to the Jetway. Once inside the airport, they noticed quickly that people had anxious, worried looks on their faces.

The Roussels had rented a private car so they went outside the terminal to find their driver. It was an absolute mob scene, people everywhere, cabs and cars honking their horns. It quickly became obvious they weren't going to find their driver and car.

So into their lives came Azim, who had a Lincoln Town Car for hire. They exited the airport at a pretty good clip but could see the traffic building up. When they got to Queens, Azim was resourceful and zig-zagged a lot to keep moving. Then they came to a standstill. Azim's radio was on and by then, everybody realized how bad things were. And there was no way you couldn't think about 9/11.

He got them to within a block of the up ramp of the 59th Street Bridge over the East River. It was 7 p.m. The radio had reported sunset was at 7:56 p.m.

"You need to walk," Azim told them.

"I was flabbergasted," said Linda, "but he knew it was the only way we could make it to the Plaza before dark. He was really a good guy."

They took what bags they could and Azim said he would get the rest of the luggage to them the next day. A large tip encouraged him to do just that. Then, like an overprotective parent admonishing a couple of kids, Azim said, "Don't worry – I'll stay and watch you get onto the bridge."

"Of course he would," Linda said. "There was no way he could move his car."

Thus the great adventure began. Of the thousands and thousands on the bridge, 97 percent were going west toward Queens. "We were part of that elite 3 percent heading east," she said.

With helicopters flying overhead, it was a painful, uphill climb to the top but they got there. "It felt good because my muscles were burning," she said. At the bottom of the bridge, they had to negotiate a barricade and chain link fence, but, hey, the end was in sight. They got off the bridge, saw private citizens directing traffic, and found their way to the Plaza at Fifth Avenue and 59th.

They had walked about an hour and a quarter – with luggage. The Plaza had set up a generator outside on 59th (Central Park West) so huge lights could shine in the reception area. They couldn't check in because the computers were down. They got a key to get in and out of the hotel.

Misery loves company, they say. They ran into a family from Clearwater, Florida, who came to New York for a wedding. And what a wedding it must have been. Candlelight, anyone?

The Roussels' diet for the day had included coffee, two airline-sized bags of pretzels and two soft drinks. So they went into the Oak Bar to get a libation. There were candles everywhere and it was getting warm. But they soon got some food: Ham, Swiss cheese and brown bread, no mustard. "My birthday dinner was compliments of the Plaza," Linda said. "It was very dry but we wolfed it down."

The hotel finally got one elevator working and began taking people up in convoys, one floor at a time. They got their room, 1214, but discovered on the way up that their key said 1241. "Let me say this. The hotel people were frazzled, but they could not have been more professional," she said.

Room 1241 turned out to be a suite, which they did not request. "It's pitch black, I can't see a thing," said Linda. So she pulled out her cigarette lighter and saw a bed with a pair of shoes on it. "They were cute, but not my size."

Finally they got into their room, 1214. The toilets flushed but there was no hot water. "Every time I started to sleep," she said, "I started laughing. What else could you do?"

Praise the Lord — the next morning miraculously found the air conditioning on. "I'll never complain about being cold again in my life.", she said. Her flowers arrived, they were beautiful and Azim faithfully delivered the clothes. Off they went to explore New York.

Richard was worried about money because credit cards were useless. They found a working ATM that still had cash and got some. Rockefeller Center? Nothing doing there. Closed. St. Patrick's Church? Even though it was a Holy Day of Obligation (Assumption of the Blessed Virgin Mary), a sign there read: "Church closed. No Mass. No lights." You couldn't even pray. No subways, no trains, no shopping.

"It was an eerie feeling," said Richard, "watching all these ladies walking down Fifth Avenue and not being able to shop — and the men probably saying, 'Thank you, Lord.' "

They got to Chanterelle Restaurant in Tribeca that Friday night and had "a delightful dinner." They looked forward to Saturday, the day they figured, "we're going to get to do something."

No such luck. One of Linda's missions was to get to Century 21, the world's largest discount department store near Ground Zero. She got there but didn't last 10 minutes. "It was hot and all you could smell was body odor. Most of New York did not have hot water. It was stifling."

They tried to get to the 42nd Street Photo store but in the heat, they got confused and walked totally in the wrong direction. They tried to see if the oyster bar at Grand Central Station was open. It was not. Museums? As Noo Yawkers say, fuggedaboutit. So they went back to the coolest place, their hotel.

Dinner at the Gramercy Tavern was good but the restaurant was warm. On Sunday they finally got to church. And at 3 p.m. they took a cab to LaGuardia Airport for their 5:30 flight home.

This time they checked their baggage. "I wasn't going through that again," Linda said.

Murphy's Law states that, "When things just can't get any worse, they will." They soon learned that their flight back home through Pittsburgh had been canceled and their bags dumped. They found a 9 p.m. flight to Charlotte, N.C., where they would spend the night and fly home Monday. The flight, of course, was two hours late.

They checked into a hotel at 1:30 a.m. and got a 5:45 a.m. wake-up call. The rest is history they'd rather forget.

"I guess the highlight is the way New Yorkers handled it," said Richard. "I think 9/11 changed the whole city forever. There were no reports of crime, no looting, no panic. People walked calmly, there was no running or pushing."

"I'll go back but not anytime soon," said Linda. "It was a trip where I did nothing that I'd ever done before and nothing I ever want to do again."

The blackout atmosphere, she said, "is different from a hurricane scene. You don't have a roof that's disappeared. There's no tree blocking the street. You can walk outside. But it's just total inconvenience."

There are a lot of memories the Roussels will take with them, but one stands out in the birthday girl's mind.

"In New York City, you could look up and see the Big Dipper," she said. "I've never seen a single star there before. You couldn't see the

Empire State Building, but you could see the Big Dipper."

A rare moment indeed in pitch-black New York – but a moment they'd never want to experience again.

The Vacation From Hell, Texas-Style

July 12, 2002

The Clapper family was excited about their first vacation in quite some time. They were going to stay in a cabin at Yogi Bear's Jellystone Park and spend most of their time at Schlitterbahn, definitely a word you don't want to try to pronounce after a few drinks.

If you don't know what Schlitterbahn is, many people think it is one of the best mega-water parks in the country, featuring a variety of attractions including tortuous, death-defying rides, one through pitch-dark chutes. They have names like Master Blaster, Raging River Tube Chute and Torrent Wave River.

Remember those last two names.

Reuben Clapper, wife Linda, their teen-age girls Wendy and Tara and his brother-in-law's family of Bill, Cindy and Brittany Fleet left New Orleans on the Sunday before July Fourth. Anticipation was high as they hit the road in two vans. Everything had been pre-paid and their cabin awaited them . . .

In Bandera, Texas, just northwest of San Antonio in Texas Hill Country.

If you've kept up with the news then you know that it was not, shall we say, a good week to be anywhere near that area.

The group never got close to Schlitterbahn in nearby New Braunfels but they certainly had a Raging River ride of their own they will never forget.

"We got in and it was sprinkling a little," said Reuben Clapper, a mechanic for Emile Virgadamo's auto repair shop on Airline Highway in New Orleans. The shop had been extremely busy lately and Clapper had volunteered to forego his vacation and send his wife and kids by themselves. But Virgadamo insisted he go because his employee had been putting in long hours.

"They told us it hadn't rained since May," said Clapper. Sunday was a lousy day but they walked around and got the lay of the land, took a look at the little brook the kids could tube in and frankly, he said, it was disappointing because there wasn't enough water.

That would change quickly.

Monday was another lousy day so they stayed in and figured Tuesday would be better. When Clapper woke up Tuesday morning he heard the sound of rain again and for a moment thought about going back to sleep. Instead he got up to take a look outside.

"That little brook wasn't a brook anymore," he said. "It had turned into a river and the picnic tables were under water."

"That water's coming up fast," said his wife.

Truer words were never spoken. Visitors were starting to move their cars and campers to higher ground, so Clapper went down to the office to see what he could find out. The office said no evacuation orders had yet been given, but the fire department arrived and told everyone that if they heard a horn blow to get in their cars and drive out.

Clapper was gone about 35 minutes. When he got back to his cabin, he saw other cabins starting to move, freed from their foundations. He grabbed his camera and began to shoot pictures. He saw a floating cabin collide with another cabin.

The Clappers and the Fleets started throwing things in their vehicles as fast as they could. The water was coming up over the tires. But where would they go? The bridge over the river is 27 feet from the ground below it, Clapper said, and the day before they had walked under the bridge. Now water was covering the bridge.

They were getting a lot of mixed signals. Then a fireman told them to hurry up and get out because "we've got an eight-foot wall of water coming down the river." Not exactly words you want to hear.

"I was scared," said Clapper, who saw some cars gambling with the ride over the bridge and decided to follow suit. "I saw a couple cars go and I said, whoa – that's it, we're outta here." The bridge was closed shortly afterwards.

They finally got to higher ground and when they did, he said, "We gave each other a hug. God forbid if we hadn't gotten out."

"I've never seen water come up so fast," he said. "There was no water under that bridge on Sunday. Inner tubes would have hit the ground. I've been around water all my life. I'm from Cape Cod. I've seen water come up – but not like that. It looked like an ocean. Water as far as the eye could see."

He called his auto repair shop and before he could say a word, Virgadamo said, "I bet you got a wet butt." He had been watching the Texas flood reports on CNN.

Some four million people in 24 counties have been affected, nine are known dead at this writing, and the property damage could reach $1 billion with houses and businesses full of muddy water, uprooted trees everywhere and a large cleanup ahead.

The Clappers and the Fleets drove their two vehicles straight home, all the way to New Orleans, getting in about 2:30 a.m. Wednesday morning. But not before they got pulled over by Texas highway patrolmen. Clapper told his story and the officer said, "You all have been through a lot, but take it easy." He let them go without a speeding ticket. "I was so glad to get home," Clapper said, "and I don't even like the place we live in."

As vacations go, it was a total bummer – the kind of thing you'd expect from Clark Griswold in "National Lampoon's Vacation." So when they got back, they took the girls to the Riverwalk and gave them each $100 to have some fun. It was a nice try but it certainly wasn't Schlitterbahn.

With vacations like that, said Clapper, "Work looks pretty good. You better believe it.

"It was amazing. It went from a brook to a stream to a river to an ocean," he said, still shaking his head in disbelief more than a week later. And one of his last memories, he said, was big old plastic Yogi Bear floating downstream.

That day he was not saying, "Hey, Boo-Boo! Pic-a-nic baskets."

CHAPTER 6
Eatin' and Drinkin'

Rock 'N' Bowl Will Never Die

July 20, 2003

John Blancher, owner of world-famous Mid-City Lanes Rock 'N' Bowl, finished reading the newspaper article and just smiled.

A story in USA Today this past Tuesday revealed that a trendy new Hollywood nightspot, Lucky Strike Lanes, came up with the idea of turning a bowling alley into a hangout for hipsters. The lanes, the story said, bills itself as America's first "bowling lounge" with a retro feel.

So, I asked the owner, what's been going on at Rock 'N' Bowl all these years?

"If it happened in California, I guess it had to be first," joked the affable Blancher, who has operated the highly successful and unique late-hours combination music and bowling Mecca since 1988 – which last time I checked came before 2003.

Mid-City Lanes opened in 1941. When Blancher bought it in 1988, the colors and design, he said, were something straight out of 1958. "It's definitely retro," he said of his place. "And I would guess mine looks more retro than theirs because mine's the real deal. I didn't design it – that's just the way it was." And the way it is.

Rock 'N' Bowl has a national reputation that lures convention-eers, vacation visitors to the city, TV and movie stars, musicians and other celebs. "There's a whole lot of people from L.A. and California who've been in my place and said, 'I wish you'd open up a place like this in my hometown,'" Blancher said.

But that's not his style. "I just try to maintain the uniqueness of what we have. The whole evolution of Rock 'N' Bowl was not me sitting down and saying we're gonna do this and we're gonna do that."

In fact, Blancher will tell you he was flying by the seat of his pants when he bought the place and half his family thought he was nuts to do so. But earlier that year Blancher had made a trip to Medjugorje, Yugoslavia, where many believers seek spiritual renewal. There he left a note on an altar asking that he find something in life in which his whole family could get involved.

Things started extremely slowly back then but by 1993 it had picked up. In June of 1993 he decided to start a zydeco night every Thursday along with ladies night. He also added "The Happy Bowlers," a league for the mentally handicapped. He felt there was a void, a need for these things.

One Thursday in October of '93, someone didn't show up for work and Blancher found himself behind the bar. As he tells it, a guy in his mid-50s with a scraggly gray beard, and wearing cutoffs, a T-shirt and sandals came in and ordered an alligator po-boy.

"You're not from here, are you?" asked Blancher. The man replied that no, he wasn't but how did Blancher know? "Locals don't eat alligator po-boys, tourists do," he responded. Blancher got busy, didn't talk to the guy any more and before long Rockin' Dopsie was bringing his gear in for a show.

"We had a big crowd and it was a great night," Blancher recalled. "When Dopsie came in, he told me there was a writer from National Geographic in the house and I should meet him."

Well, the writer turned out to be the guy with the scraggly beard and Blancher found out he had been sent to New Orleans for five months to do an in-depth piece on the city for the January, 1995 issue – because New Orleans had the Super Bowl, Final Four, Mardi Gras and the Jazzfest all lined up that year.

Just to show you how things happen, and one of the reasons Blancher is so deeply religious and a believer in fate, is how the writer wound up at Rock 'N' Bowl. "He couldn't get a room downtown," said Blancher, "so he wound up at the Quality Inn on Tulane Avenue. Their restaurant was closed so they sent him across the street to Home Plate Inn. Their restaurant was also closed, so they sent him to my place."

The writer came back every Thursday night for the five months he was in New Orleans. "What happens here on Thursday night I don't think you can see anywhere else in the world – black Cajun cowboys wearing boots and cowboy hats dancing to this unique music," said Blancher. That, plus ladies night and "The Happy Bowlers" league.

The writer wound up interviewing Blancher about how bizarre this bowling alley-music combo establishment was. "He thought it was a cultural phenomenon," said Blancher. When the National Geographic issue came out in January of 1995, it had a 19-page story on New Orleans with an entire page devoted to Rock 'N' Bowl.

That opened the media floodgates. Blancher said CNN did something in February, USA Today a story in March. In April it was Life Magazine's turn, Rolling Stone did a piece that appeared in June, which was followed by a seven-minute segment on "The Today Show."

All because a couple of restaurants were closed.

The new hot spot in California may well be a hangout for celebs, but there has been no shortage of them at Rock 'N' Bowl. Tom Cruise, Nicole Kidman, Susan Sarandon, Ashley Judd, Sharon Osbourne, John Goodman, Julia Roberts, Tim Robbins, Brad Pitt and one of Blancher's favorites, Weird Al Yankovic, just to name a few, have all spent quality time there.

There have been two weddings there, and ten receptions, including those of Blancher's son and daughter, who both work with him in the business, which includes his newly-purchased Ye Olde College Inn.

Blancher couldn't care less if some nouveau Hollywood bowling hot spot is billed as the first of its kind. He would rather tell you about how he and his wife Debbie and his entire family have been extremely blessed and why he has hosted countless benefits for musicians. Last Sunday night, he hosted a benefit to raise money for a cemetery tomb for local musicians whose families cannot afford them.

But possibly his favorite pastime is to regale a crowd with stories about strange things that have happened there. Around 1989 or '90, he said, Tulane University was hosting some Tibetan monks who were doing a chanting exhibition.

About four or five of them came climbing up the lengthy and steep set of steps that get you from the ground to the second floor, where the bowling alley is located. He said one of them told him, "We were walking down Carrollton Avenue and saw the big bowling pin outside." Blancher said they told him they like to try everything once and had never bowled before.

They had on their robes and were barefoot and did not want bowling shoes. "Just don't drop it on your foot," Blancher told them. He's sorry he didn't take any pictures, he said, because it might have been a good promotion.

"Just think," he said, "people from all over the world climb the mountains of Tibet to ask them about the meaning of life. I could have said the monks climbed the steps of Rock 'N' Bowl to find out what bowling to music is all about."

(Rock 'N' Bowl moved to its new location at Carrollton Avenue and Earhart Boulevard next to Ye Olde College Inn in the spring of 2009. It has retained its retro atmosphere.)

The Rebirth of the Parkway Bakery

October 22, 2003

In a city where fashionably decadent architecture, rusting lace ironwork balconies, peeling paint, ferns growing in gutters and stylish seeds of decline are revered, the Parkway Bakery at North Hagan and Toulouse streets took the ambiance of decay to another level.

Long after the sloppy po-boy restaurant closed its doors in the mid-'90s, many a carload of hungry bettors and Jazzfest-goers in search of a fried ham and cheese po-boy would ignore the collapsing roof and the peeling paint – after all, the place had always looked that way – and knock on the screen door where there was that hand-lettered sign that said: "No one allowed inside without a shirt."

For years they left disappointed. But no more. The new Parkway has been lovingly restored by contractor Jay Nix, and the restaurant that was once a wrecking ball candidate is now one of the most incredible comeback corners in the city.

A man walked by the other day and said, "This guy ain't a contractor – he's David Copperfield."

In the old days, the Parkway baked its own bread in two huge brick ovens, sending a familiar and tempting aroma throughout the area near the brake tag station and Bayou St. John. The restaurant kept long hours, generally from 6 a.m. to 11:30 p.m., seven days a week except holidays. Brothers Bubby and Jake Timothy took it over from their dad, who bought it in 1922 when it was a bakery. In 1932, it started making sandwiches.

Bubby and Jake wouldn't win any hospitality awards, nor would the Parkway get any good housekeeping commendations. What they did do was make great sandwiches, so the hordes descended on the tiny eatery famed for its sloppy roast beefs.

Among them were many of the 1,500 workers from the nearby American Can Company, cab drivers, firemen, cops, politicians, racetrack railbirds, waiters and bartenders from the French Quarter, employees from the neighboring funeral home, doctors, nurses and staff of Mercy Hospital, brake tag station inspectors and countless more, running the social gamut from the hard-hat and blue-collar crowd to Uptown bluebloods.

You could even knock on the door after hours and get in.

"We'd finish up at Lenfant's where we were playing with the Basin Street Six," said Pete Fountain, "and we'd go get hot bread from the baker, Mr. Tom, at 2 or 3 in the morning. The gravy would be cooking for the next day. Then he'd get out the roast beef and we'd eat. The roast beef was the living end, all that gravy and mayo."

Sam Clesi, co-owner of nearby R&S Auto Service, recalled a big vat filled with gravy that had a water spigot. "I was fascinated with that. They'd turn the spigot, pass the sandwich underneath it for extra gravy. Think about it, a water valve with gravy coming out."

Thirty years ago, the roast beef po-boy cost 75 cents. Dressed, 10 cents more. The fried ham and cheese was one of the more expensive items. Dressed, it was $1.30. The oyster sandwich was a buck. Barq's and beer were the most popular drinks.

As for the brothers, one had slightly more personality than the other. That would be Jake. Bubby would growl at you. But then in New Orleans, that sort of behavior has always been embraced as local color.

After years of neglect, declining business and long past its prime, the Parkway closed. It was purchased by Nix who had bought other property in that same block and had a vision for the place. Not long after he took control, he put up a small sign on a post that read, "We're Saving Parkway."

But he didn't save it right away.

"I picked at it. I didn't have any money to do anything," he said. Over a couple of years, he took down the jerry-rigged pile of rubble that was a lean-to and some of the most patched-up, bubble-gummed, Band-Aided layers of "architecture" ever known to man. "They had stuck 4X4s in there to hold it up and keep the ceiling from coming down."

He found grease an inch thick on the baseboards and on the doors and walls he found coat after coat of paint.

It took Nix more than 20 Dumpster loads to haul off the rubble. And then he took apart the ovens, brick by brick. The ovens hadn't worked since the 1978 flood; still hot from use, the bricks had cracked when floodwater reached the ovens.

Nix sold 20,000-plus bricks from classic old brickyards like Pelican, Columbia and Jaxon for 50 cents apiece, raising about $10,000 for the renovation.

The building, which likely dates to near the turn of the century, has been classically restored, in and out, and is a distinctive mix of Art Deco, Caribbean, and very New Orleans influences. The doors and window sills are painted Black Forest green. The shutters are classic burgundy. The body and weatherboards are golden mustard, and the trim is a very light pale yellow.

Ray St. Pierre, the other co-owner of R&S Auto Service, told Nix, "I know how you picked the outside colors."

"How?" asked Nix.

"For ketchup, mustard and mayonnaise," he answered.

"What about the green?"

"That's for pickles," said Noel Clesi, Sam's wife.

"You know, they're right," said Nix. "I wish I had planned it that way."

On the front of the building, there are three marquee signs, the kind you used to see on mom and pop groceries and bars and restaurants all over town. The sign facing Toulouse says, "Beer & Po-Boys." The sign over the entrance reads: "Parkway Bakery & Tavern." And the sign facing North Hagan says simply: "Good Food. Cocktails."

"When you approach the building," Nix said, "you feel like you're back in the '50s." Indeed you do. You can almost imagine walking three blocks north on Hagan and going to the Imperial Theater to see "Roman Holiday" with Audrey Hepburn and Gregory Peck.

"And when you go inside," Nix continued, "you go back another 50 years." The dark, intricate floor-to-ceiling wooden bar that looks like it was pulled from another old tavern was actually built from scratch by Nix's crew. It resembles the bar at the Napoleon House and the bar at Carrollton Station on Willow Street.

The new Parkway bar also provides a scenic view of Bayou St. John and in the background, the old American Can Company, now renovated into The Bakery Condominiums.

Inside, all the old millwork, the transoms, the wainscoting, the very rare raised fluted panel doors were stripped and repainted. An "old school flooring" of exposed aggregate was poured new to make it look old. The seating area where three cramped tables dwelled is no more. The back of the restaurant, which customers never saw, has been opened up and will be an L-shaped seating area.

Nix added classic old shutters, eye-catching rooster cone convection vents on the roof (which he calls "Wizard of Oz" vents), outdoor seating underneath a reconstructed lean-to, a parking lot with bright lighting and all the modern kitchen technology available — including a six-burner stove, a conventional oven, a 4-foot char-broiler, three fryers and more.

"Old place, new face," Nix said. "It started out as a renovation and became a restoration. The same four guys that have worked with me for years did all of this. The place is legendary, really, and that motivated me. I have this eye for restoration – that's what we do best, and once I start I can't hold back. You can see that in the attention to detail. I probably could have cut tons of corners but I couldn't bring myself to do that."

As for the cuisine, it'll be what was there before and more: 12 traditional po-boys, including roast beef, hot sausage, oysters, shrimp, fried ham, turkey, ham and cheese, hamburgers, cheeseburgers, even French fry po-boys. Customers will place an order at the service window, get themselves a drink and wait for their numbers to be called.

"This is not fine dining," Nix said. "This is low dollar, high volume stuff. Po-boys were created during the worst economy this nation ever had, the Depression. We're not doing $8 po-boys here. The people who live around here are all working class people. They drive pickup trucks, they get up and go to work every day and they don't have much time for lunch."

Ever since the renovation started in July, the rubber-necking from motorists has been constant. "The building really slaps you in the face when you drive by," he said. But even though you can look in his eyes and see how satisfied he is with his effort, he's hardly taking anything for granted.

"This isn't K&B or Krauss coming back. This is more like Royal Castle coming back. I've got a vision and it's coming together. Normally when you go into the restaurant business people tell you that you're nuts. Nobody's saying that.

"Everybody who sees it tells me it's a grand slam home run. But I can't get caught up in that hype. I'm opening it like it's failing. But that's just my nature."

And just in case he needs some divine intervention, Nix put

aside something for that. "With the remainder of those bricks I'm making a little shrine," he said, pointing to an outside corner behind the office where a religious figure hangs on a wall. "So I can pray I do well."

(The new Parkway Bakery, despite the owner's doubts, has been an enormous success.)

Domilise's: Change Is Not on the Menu

March 21, 2004

They walked in through the unimposing door at the corner of Annunciation and Bellecastle streets just as they had done 20 years before when they were students at Tulane University.

The same "Domilise's Po-Boy & Bar" neon sign still graced the entranceway as it has for as long as anyone can remember.

The men, now in their 40s, were in town this past year for their 20th college reunion and a po-boy from Domilise's was on their "must do" list.

"I was over there slicing roasts and these two gentlemen walked in," said Dot Domilise, briefly off her feet for 15 minutes of her typical 12-hour day and telling some tales. "Then one of them said to the other, 'This place hasn't changed at all.' "

Then he turned around and saw Dot Domilise's face. Their eyes met. "You're still here?" he said incredulously.

"Where did you want me to be?" she shot back. She said the look of astonishment on his face, his jaw hanging open, caused her to "almost cut my hand in the meat slicer."

But that's the way it is and that's the way it always has been at Domilise's. Same roast beef, fried oyster and fried shrimp po-boys, same simple tables, same fresh baked local French bread, same frosty schooners of beer, same faces and one of the friendliest places you've ever been.

"I don't believe in change," said Domilise, stating the obvious. "If it works, don't change it. In 20 years it's still gonna be the same if I'm here."

And why shouldn't she be? Right now she's just a kid of 81 years who has been behind the counter since 1947 – and wearing her years in a fashion that any 60-year-old would kill for. Her bartender, Raymond Chauvin, however, is just a rookie.

"Raymond, how long you been here?" she asked.

"Thirty-four years, but I don't know if I'm gonna stay," he said. "I'm gonna think about it a few more years."

There's an old Sicilian proverb that states, "The less things change, the more they remain the same." But sometimes change is unavoidable, even at Domilise's.

Late last year, one of the shop's specialty items came to the end of the road. For almost a quarter of a century, pepper weiner po-boys had been a hot item. Not to be confused with hot sausage, the pepper weiner, said Domilise, "was a different kind of meat. Its taste was not like a weiner taste. It was flavored to be hot but there were no cut-up seasonings visible, just plain meat in a casing."

At one time the casings were edible but then they got tougher, so they were painstakingly peeled off. But the effort was worth it, as far as the product's fans were concerned. "There were people who once they tried them and liked them, that's all they ordered," Domilise said.

But then supplier after supplier bit the dust, manufacturers quit making them and try as she might, she can't find anything even remotely similar in taste to replace them. "I've tried a lot of 'hot franks,' as they call them but none of them are any good," she said.

So they're off the menu board but far from being out of people's minds. They're now just the missing link. "Domilise's without pepper weenies is like a roast beef po-boy without gravy," said longtime customer Joe Puglia.

Dot Domilise said customers ordering sandwiches to go over the phone have hung up on her when she broke the news. "I tell them we can't get them and the receiver goes down," she said.

People have come in from out of town just for that item only to be terribly disappointed. They have big smiles when they step up to the counter and place their orders. Then she has to say, "When I tell you what I'm about to tell you, that smile's gonna come off your face." Especially with a such a large menu, Domilise said, "It surprises me that something like that meant so much." But on closer review, like her, her customers aren't used to change.

The business was opened more than 75 years ago by her father-in-law, Peter Domilise, who came here from Italy and bought what had been a dry goods store. He dropped the floor of the front of the camelback house to street level, opened a bar, and created a place where people of the neighborhood could congregate, Dot said. The sandwiches came a little later.

But things didn't take off until the riverfront, only a couple blocks away, became a steady place to work.

Originally from Franklin, La., she married Peter's son, Sam, in 1943, and after a week of marriage, his Army anti-aircraft unit was sent overseas. After he returned, they began working in the business in 1947. But Sam quickly became more involved in local politics and Carnival, serving as the captain of the Krewe of Thoth for 28 years before his death in 1980.

And always holding sway behind the counter was Dot, these days alongside her daughter-in-law, Patti Domilise. "I couldn't do it without her, no way," she said. "And I've got some other ladies that come in."

One year turns into 10 and quickly into . . . 57 years?

"It's my social world. I don't know what I would do without this place," Dot Domilise said, eyeballing the photos of regulars that adorn the walls. Her visitor got up to check them out.

"You're gonna see mostly Dennis Waldron (Criminal District Court Judge Waldron) up there 'cause he's in charge of that wall, he tells me," she said with a wry smile. But there are many, many others. All the Manning boys and Archie. James Rivers and Clint Eastwood. Banu Gibson. Former U.S. Rep. Bob Livingston. Phil Harris and Alice Faye.

There are also countless pictures of high school kids. "Some of those kids that came in here when they were schoolkids – mostly

Newman, Sacred Heart, Tulane and Loyola kids – they grow up and their kids get married and I get invited," she said.

All in the family, as they say.

Domilise stared out the door that so many thousands of Orleanians have walked through. "Yesterday we had people standing out the door lined up. Today not that much. But the bread man tells me it's like that all over," she said with a knowing look.

A knowing look that said it's happened before, it'll happen again, and the less things change, the more they stay the same.

An Uptown Drinking Establishment Since 1934

October 23, 1994

Stephanie Bruno sat at a table this week inside an Uptown institution her late father began 60 years ago. She took one look at an old photo of him dressed up in a devil's costume with horns and a tail, bushier-than-usual eyebrows, bulging eyes behind oversized glasses and a cigar that made him look like one of the Marx brothers.

Then she offered this simple, understated memory:

"He was more of a character than anybody ever knew or ever will."

The late Leo Bruno, who opened Bruno's College Inn on Maple Street in 1934, was certainly that. He began a legend and tradition that not just lives, but thrives. At the corner of Maple and Hillary streets, Bruno's remains THE gathering spot for thirsty Tulane students, alumni, parents and grandparents, and University-area Uptowners.

Each year Bruno reigned as king of his own mock Carnival ball, the BBB, or Babbling Bastards of Bruno's. Leo was King Leo for Life, but the queen and her court were selected from debs who frequented the bar late at night during debutante and Carnival seasons. He rented mule-drawn oyster or banana wagons for his parade, held the queen's supper across the street at the Maple Hill restaurant, and paraded from Maple and Hillary streets late at night through the surrounding neighborhood.

"When I was a young kid, they let me stay up to see it," said Bruno. "I didn't know what to expect. I guess I expected Rex, or Momus. What I saw was my dad on some stupid-looking forklift with some plywood something or other around him and a bunch of wagons following. After it passed, I said, 'What was that?' "

As she grew older, Stephanie Bruno would understand exactly what it was, some sort of predecessor to today's funky Krewe du Vieux parade in the French Quarter. "This was the kooky counter-culture parade, and for a lot of the debs, it was almost more gratifying being in this than Comus or Momus," she said.

To honor the historic six-decade anniversary, David Melius – who has owned Bruno's since 1983 – and his wife, Selby Schonekas Melius, are holding a week-long celebration.

One of the great memories for virtually all customers is bartender Big George Rankin, a muscular ex-boxer and semi-pro baseball player who was with Leo since Day One. Rankin, who died some years ago, was a well-liked, perceptive, philosophic man with a great sense of humor who had a superb memory for names. Through the years he served such luminaries as former District Attorney Jim Garrison, defense lawyer F. Irvin Dymond, many of the Ochsner medical clan, countless lawyers, doctors, judges and politicos, and even Sonny and Cher, who stopped in one day for a thirst-quencher.

Inside the brick walls with beamed ceilings, rich dark paneling, double fireplace and coach lights, all the bartenders wore starched green vests, white shirts and black bow ties. The jukebox remained virtually unchanged for 25 years, with music such as "Bolero" on it, in memory of a young woman who could not resist stripping to it when it was played late at night and she had downed enough 151-proof rum.

"We kept it on there for a while out of deference to our patrons," David Melius said. "But one night somebody played it and I lost my whole crowd. Tradition is great but you have got to change with the times." So out went Ravel and "Bolero" and in came Garth Brooks, Paul Simon and tunes people heard on the radio, not in music appreciation classes.

The most visible figure of all, however, was the portly, nattily-attired Bruno, always perched on a stool next to the Hillary Street entrance, his elbow on the jukebox, a large cigar in hand. He looked like a friendly poppa frog on a lily pad.

"I've heard all the stories," said Stephanie Bruno, a public relations executive. "He and George were an unusual pair, perfectly suited for each other. They were both originals and constantly clashed. Daddy must have fired him a hundred times and George came back a hundred times. They were both entertainers and really needed each other."

Bruno's didn't have a closing hour. It just shut down when the crowd got sparse. "I know he used to drive the kids home he didn't think could drive home, he took them out to eat at his best friend Sam Domino's pizza restaurant downtown, he counseled many people, and got a few of them out of jail. He wouldn't get in until dawn but it was truly a lifestyle that suited him."

Bruno and his barflies loved Tulane and Tulane athletics, a tradition that carries on today. When Bruno's opened, Tulane was months away from playing in the inaugural Sugar Bowl in 1935 vs. Temple, which the Green Wave would win, 20-14. Monday morning quarterbacks and second guessers of all Tulane sports events still gather there.

"We were genuinely thrilled when David bought Bruno's," Stephanie Bruno said. "He had an affection for the old Bruno's that made it dear to so many people. There are thousands of bars you can go into in New Orleans but Bruno's was always like a club. My dad realized that and David realizes it. It's a place you can go and always see people you know – and that's what sets it apart from the other thousands of bars in New Orleans. Generations of the same families came in there and still do."

One story that a lot of today's Bruno's crowd may not know was told to me by Big George Rankin. When Leo Bruno opened the place in 1934, his partner was none other than Pat O'Brien. After a couple of successful years, O'Brien wanted to move the business to the French Quarter but Bruno didn't want to leave what he called "the college belt."

They decided to split, as friends. As Rankin told me years later, with no regrets, "Leo made a fair and decent and honest living, and so did I, while Pat went down to the Quarter and made a goddamn fortune."

(New Bruno's is now located at 7538 Maple St., catty-corner from the location when this story was written.)

Bars on Memory Lane

July 18, 2008

Acy's Hoedown was a wonderfully seedy, decadent and spacious dance and pool hall with enormously high ceilings. It also had swinging front doors like a saloon in an old cowboy movie – scratched and scarred and kicked-in many times.

Located on Sophie Wright Place, a two-block stretch just off Magazine and St. Andrew streets, it attracted such country legends as Ernest Tubb and the Texas Troubadors. There is a memory of a glorious night in the mid-'60s when a bunch of customers stood on plywood on top of pool tables to get a glimpse of Tubb and pals singing "Walking the Floor Over You."

The building the dance hall occupied dates back to the 1850s and, so the story goes, was once a notorious gambling hall. In the 1970s it changed hands and became known as Acy's Pool Hall, more famous for its sloppy roast beef po-boys than western swing. Like most bars, it eventually shuttered its swinging doors and the music died.

Ah, bars long gone. So many of them, so little time. While you're checking out today's "Lagniappe Bar Guide: 75 Great Places to Drink," mapping out and personalizing your pub crawl, think about some of these long-gone watering holes . . .

Like La Casa de Los Marinos, a rough and tumble Latin sea-man's bar at the corner of Toulouse and Decatur streets, where Café Maspero is today. It was edgy before edgy was coined.

La Casa, as it was known, was unique because it was three bars in one. The first bar was the most populated and the most touristy. If you were adventurous, you'd move into what some called the "cat-acombs," the second and third bars. The second bar was consider-ably more rowdy, and the third bar, dark as night, where there was always live Latin music and dancing, you entered at your own risk. The crowd I hung with liked live music.

If you preferred a Greek seaman's hangout, there was the Acropolis, a short distance away on Decatur. They did the famous dance long before "Zorba" hit the screen.

Curley's Neutral Corner (and gym) in my lifetime was first located at Poydras and St. Charles, and then at Carondelet and Poydras. A plush hangout for the "write and fight" crowd, the orig-inal location featured a regulation boxing ring where newspaper writers gathered after hours – sometimes during hours – to drink and watch fighters spar with each other. There was late-night live music.

Conceived and funded by boxing promoter Blaise D'Antoni and operated by Alphonse "Curley" Gagliano, a bald-headed former boxer whose establishment also attracted politicos, bookmakers and horseplayers, it attracted such world champion boxers as Willie Pastrano and Ralph Dupas. Curley's was made famous in A.J. Liebling's classic book, "The Earl of Louisiana," in which Liebling described Curley's at great length because it was the headquarters for gubernatorial candidate Allen "Black Cat" LaCombe – boxing pro-moter and handicapper — running against Earl Long.

Out at the lakefront on West End Boulevard at the marina was Bart's, gone before Katrina, but it lingers in my memory because of many a late afternoon and evening watching boats dock and sail-boats on their way into the lake as the sun went down. Its clientele included Coast Guardsmen from the nearby station, U.S. Navy and Marine reservists, yacht clubbers, boaters, Lakeview residents, the early Saints players and anybody who wanted to unwind at a water-front setting.

The nearby Porthole also provided a great view.

Bars through the years have provided an environment for human interaction like nothing else. They are museums of memories, special moments, characters and good times. But bars come and go, and some more of the lost include:

Eight Sons Lounge on Franklin Avenue just off Robert E. Lee with that mural of the Milneburg area, run by the Puglisi brothers. Pat Gillen's on Metairie Road, a great vantage point for many a St. Patrick's Day parade. The Silver Eagle on Belle Chasse Highway for country-western music. Cusimano's at Prytania and Robert streets with its orange booths. Graffagnino's Tavern, at Laurel and Calhoun, run by Lola and Jake Graffagnino and famed for its St. Patrick's Day parties. Liquid Assets and the Variety Stag Bar in the CBD. Home Plate Inn on Tulane Avenue, across from old Pelican Stadium.

Quasimodo's on Carrollton Avenue at Riverbend, with that great motto: "Does Quasimodo ring a bell?" Larry & Katz on Cleveland Avenue, where you sat on beer cases and never got carded. The Belfort Inn near the Fair Grounds, Four Kins on Danneel Street, later the Red Lion, now the Neutral Ground Coffee House. Norby's on Webster and Laurel, home of the Tulane-LSU wheelbarrow races, now held at Henry's Bar on Magazine Street.

The Rest-A-While, a great name and if memory serves, it was on Dreux Street in a basement with a bunch of benches and rocking chairs. Jed's University Inn on Lowerline Street, near the Tulane campus. The Rendon Inn with its ice cold frozen beer schooners. Beachball Benny's, once Munster's by the Wisner Playground. The Webster Street bar, later AT II, now Monkey Hill. Fee's on Jospeh Street.

The late great Bonn-A-Bell on Aurora Street, now the Electric Cocktail. The Carrollton Tavern across from the Sealtest Dairy that became a post office. Quick story: A guy brought a huge sack of onions in there one night, talked everybody into stomping on them and pretty soon the place emptied – it was like tear gas in there.

Then there was Jewel's in the Quarter and Whitey's Seafood & Billiard Center on Downman Road – home of the only indoor Mardi Gras parade. Rita Bailey's on Laurel and Arabella; she wouldn't serve you, you got your own beer – she just collected. And Jimmy's on Willow Street for music.

JC's on Veterans Highway, where carhops took your order for drinks. Bronco's in Gretna, a killer country-western dance hall. And does anybody remember Le Directoire, in the Quarter, where there were telephones in each booth? Or Houlihan's, the forerunner of spots like TGIFridays, with its junque and antiques on the walls?

Maybe you do, maybe you don't. Maybe you'll recall your favorites, if they're not mentioned here. It's all just food . . . or rather, drink for thought.

(The Rendon Inn was renovated and restored in 2008, after being devastated by Hurricane Katrina.)

CHAPTER 7
Football Rules

Tulane Stadium:
Where Football Had Rah-rah-rah

October 25, 1975

Does anybody remember that late, great clock in the south end zone of Tulane Stadium that befuddled players and fans alike?

It had lighted numerals on its face that began at "14" and a horizontal bar below it with 60 markers which ticked off each second until the clock got to "0" and everybody with a brain thought the game was over.

Only it wasn't. The zero then ticked off 60 more seconds before the horn sounded, while visiting teams stood in disbelief and their coaches argued with the official clock operator that there just couldn't be time remaining after zero. And how could a quarter begin with only 14 minutes, anyway?

It was one of the great home field advantages of any football stadium I've ever been in, and during my college years at Tulane, the Greenies needed all the help they could get. From 1962 to 1966, Tulane won only six games, lost 33 and tied one.

Old grads in town for tonight's 7:30 p.m. homecoming game with Georgia Tech will undoubtedly reminisce about the lean years, but this time they won't be returning to the 80,000-seat museum of Greenie football history. Instead, they'll be inside the $163 million Superdome, a long way from the ghosts of Peggy Flournoy and Monk Simons.

You learned to appreciate the little things during the great football depression on Willow Street. You listened attentively to each public address announcement – "Doctor number 607, Westside phone at once, please," and later contemplated one of the great mysteries of life – why didn't they ever call the medics to the Eastside phone?

It was either that, or you drank a hell of a lot. I did both. My post-game condition usually lingered through Monday, seriously hindering my academic career; like the football team, at the end of my years, graduate school didn't hand me any post-season offers.

I wasn't worried, though. I had already earned the only reward I ever wanted – the coveted Green Badge of Courage – for sitting through every home game of the four worst consecutive years in Tulane football history. Not many were given out, but the badge gives you license to speak your piece about Tulane football.

Even at its 62-0 worst, college football on campus on Willow Street, where it still belongs, is what the game is all about, so help me, Terry Terrebonne.

Give me the Fenways, Crosleys and Ebbets Fields of baseball; the Dudleys, Kezars, Yale Bowls and Tulane Stadiums of football. You take the computerized, climate-controlled, symmetrical models, and I'll take the tradition, memories and history that go with the crusty misfits.

Give me the rain, the cold, the splinters in the butt, the stadium seats, cushions, sun visors, umbrellas . . . the heat, the sweat, the slippery fields, and the parking problems that go along with Tulane Stadium.

But also give me the sunshine, the moonlight, the booze and the blankets, the snuggling with your girl, the bluebird days, the Goodyear blimp, the skywriters, the portable radios buzzing with other games, the girls sun-bathing on Butler House dorm, and the skyline of New Orleans.

Give me the 1964 Sugar Bowl game that will never be forgotten, not because of the score, but because Tulane Stadium was ringed with snow from a New Year's Eve snowfall as Alabama and Ole Miss ran out on the field. And give me the electricity of a crowd of 86,958 watching Tulane beat LSU in 1973 for the first time in

25 years – the largest crowd in the history of the South.

If you think I'm prejudiced, you're right. My father spoon-fed me at age 4 on a steady diet of Eddie Price. I was hooked by the time Max McGee and Les Kennedy came along, rode my bike up and down the ramps as a 12-year-old trying to get a peek at Will Billon, and by the time I was ready to go to college, Tulane Stadium was my home away from home.

So it was with a tear in my eye and a great deal of trepidation that I went to the Superdome the first time this year, for the Ole Miss game, with the still fresh memory of placekicker Uwe Pontius lumbering onto the grass at Tulane Stadium to the cheers of "Ooohvaah! Oooh-vaah!"

What did I find? Everybody overdressed for football. No raucous, beer-drinking, oath-taking sweatshirted fans, students or otherwise. No spitting on the floor. No dogs on the field. Rules against bringing thermoses and food in the stadium. Not as many drunks.

A tamed-down, almost tranquilized crowd, confined by the roof, stifled by concession prices, waiting for the second concerto to begin, bored by loud, repetitive TV commercials, programmed to cheer by computer scoreboards, and quenching their thirsts with hermetically-sealed beer.

Less than 10 years ago, Tulane regularly advertised its stadium in its football programs as "the world's largest steel stadium, a massive double decked structure of steel and concrete" with a press box voted by writers as among the best in the nation.

Now less than a decade later, it is described as decrepit, obsolete, rusty, ready for the scrap heap. I don't believe it.

There was never anything wrong with Tulane Stadium that a few more restrooms wouldn't cure. Sure, there were parking problems, but now you just give your parking fee to some garage attendant instead of a kid on Calhoun Street trying to hustle a few dollars in his driveway.

Half the cities in the country would welcome a facility like Tulane has. I am already tired of being told by architects and Dome promoters what super sightlines the Dome has – allegedly the best anywhere. And this is hard for a Tulane fan to admit, but when it comes to sightlines, the Dome is a bad third to Tiger Stadium in Baton Rouge and Tulane.

Students on the Uptown campus are upset about being herded into buses and driven to the Dome instead of lolling down McAlister Drive, date in arm, arriving at the stadium when they want, and leaving when they want.

As might be expected, student attendance is down from 1974. If you don't want to take the bus, you can drive and pay to park. All that, with an 80,000-seat stadium a couple hundred feet from your dorm, would be hard to explain to Knute Rockne.

They say it is too expensive, maintenance-wise, for Tulane to move back to Willow Street – the steelwork needs scraping, painting and shoring up, and some seats need to be replaced. But if they ever change their minds, my chisel, scraper, paint brush and hammer are ready for action. And I am available for duty.

They Marched to Their Own Drummer

March 15, 2002

Any student of irony would tell you it was probably appropriate that the leader of Charlie's Saints Marching Club died on a Sunday – the same day of the week his favorite team succumbed on so many occasions.

Charlie Kertz was 86 when he left our fold. Whatever his official obituary will say about him, this one will call him the indefatigable leader of the most optimistic group of black and gold fans in franchise history, a man who saw more lights at the ends of more tunnels than any fan, a talkative guy who was a must interview for the media at the start of every season.

Kertz was blind and virtually deaf in his final years at home, clinging to a baby monitor that provided the only way he could hear the Saints radio broadcast and communicate with his family members.

But for years at old Tulane Stadium and after that in Section 107 of the Superdome, Charlie Kertz and his band of gold-shirted crazies partied and predicted trips to the Super Bowl, all the while providing a humanitarian service of great importance to the community.

"He was so proud of everything that the club did with the crippled children and the battered children," said daughter Joan "Sis" Serpas. Section 107 was chosen not for its sight lines but because of its proximity to the wheelchair ramp and wheelchair seating – to be near his kids.

His daughter would tell you that one of the best things about "C.K.," as he was known, was this: "He didn't act like an old man and he didn't think like an old man."

Not hardly. As one officer of the club once observed, "Charlie is living proof you can be young only once, but you can be immature your whole life."

What he was referring to, of course, were the zany shenanigans the Irish Channel-born Kertz came up with for the club's trips and parades. At the old clubhouse, Charlie's Saint House bar at Apple and Cambronne streets, the parades began when members were trying to figure out how to celebrate the team's first win in 1967.

That 31-24 victory over Philadelphia, fueled by Walter "Flea" Roberts' three touchdowns, sent Kertz and pals straight to the rocket fuel, which in turn sent their alcohol-clouded brain cells into action — and out of the kitchen came pots and pans and big spoons for beating them. One guy had a railroad flare, stuck it on a broomstick and before you could sing the first verse of "When the Saints Go Marching In," the parade tradition had begun as neighbors joined in the madness.

The parades were held only when the Saints won. So, needless to say, it wasn't exactly something you could count on. But that led to "homecoming" celebrations in which one game a year was picked out as homecoming (nobody's exactly sure who came home) and a big soiree was held.

The empty lot across the street from the bar seemed a natural spot for a bonfire, the closet pyromaniacs in the club believed. So one year a 50-foot oil well was built out of 2-by-4-foot lumber for the Houston Oilers game. Then it was doused with kerosene and set ablaze.

This story has been told before but it never really gets old. One of Kertz's best pals was former New Orleans Fire Chief William McCrossen, who was invited to witness the oil-well blaze at the bar. In his wisdom, but more likely his experience with amateur fire-bugs, the chief decided to send a fire truck along.

Just in case. Which was an excellent call on his part when the fire got out of control and the firemen had to snuff out the oil well.

"All I remember," Kertz would recall afterwards, "is all of a sudden the wind come up outta nowhere, and old man Macaluso across the street started hosing down his house with his garden hose. That's when I was glad the truck was there."

Inside the old clubhouse, painted all black and gold, there was nothing but pictures and mementos. On one wall every year was the mileage to each out-of-town game on the schedule, enticing members to make the trip. The 944 miles to Chicago one year provided a trip that was a highlight reel of things gone bad.

When the group, costumed and celebrating, was about to board the train at Union Passenger Terminal, Kertz would later tell the story, a heckler yelled, "You gotta be crazy going to Chicago to see dem bums." The train made 22 stops. Nobody slept.

When they finally got to freezing Soldier Field, they were stuck in a corner with virtually no sight lines. A Bears fan, as Bears fans will do, got drunk, dropped trou and mooned Charlie's Saints, then spilled his booze all over some of them.

"It ain't easy sticking with losers," Kertz would say time and time again. "But anybody can support a winner. To support a loser it takes something else."

Exactly what that something else is psychologists could spend years studying.

One moment that said it all about this club came back in 1973, one of the Saints' darkest moments, an opening-day 62-7 loss to Atlanta at home, in Tulane Stadium. Not a single one of the Charlie's pack left until it was over. Of course by then they were surrounded by beer vendors.

When Kertz moved his clubhouse to Maximillian's Bar in Metairie at the end of the '80s, the owner of Max's, Ronnie "The Bear" Gordy, told me: "It would be nice if this team could get to the Super Bowl before this guy starts watching it from Upstairs. He's in good shape now but who lasts forever? Nobody deserves it more than C.K."

Well, even though he was certainly deserving, wishes don't always come true. That's part of life. But along the way, C.K. lived to see and hear about his Saints making the playoffs and finally, a playoff victory came to pass.

More importantly, Charlie Kertz's vision, Charlie's Saints Marching Club, is still around and continuing to help less fortunate young Saints fans. Much as he loved them, he always said about his team, "The kids come first, the Saints come second."

Godspeed, C.K.

Karnak the Magnificent, the Sultan of Sarcasm

November 15, 2000

A first grade teacher in Baton Rouge explained to her class that she is an LSU fan. She asked her students to raise their hands if they, too, are Tiger fans.

Everyone in the class raised his hand except one little girl. The teacher looked at the girl with surprise and said, "Jenny, why didn't you raise your hand?"

"Because I'm not a Tiger fan," she answered.

The shocked teacher asked, "Well, if you are not a Tiger fan, then what are you a fan of?"

"I'm a Tulane fan," she said, "and proud of it."

The teacher was dumbfounded. After all, this was in Baton Rouge. "Why, pray tell, are you a Tulane fan?"

"Because my mom is a Tulane fan and my dad is a Tulane fan,

so I'm a Tulane fan, too!"

"Well," said the teacher, now annoyed, "that is no reason for you to be a Tulane fan. You don't have to be just like your parents all the time. What if your mom was a moron and your dad was a moron, what would you be then?"

"Then," said Jenny, "I'd be an LSU fan."

Jokes like that can mean only one thing. For the 21st consecutive year it is time to call on the keeper of mystic secrets about LSU and Tulane football.

So come in, oh Great One, the Sahib of Skepticism, the Viscount of Venom, the Sultan of Sarcasm, Karnak the Magnificent, and give us the questions inside the envelopes. Karnak, the first answer is:

A. Bridgestone-Firestone.

Q. Name the only team to suffer more blowouts than Tulane.

A. "Does this mean I passed the L.E.A.P Test?"

Q. What did the LSU student ask after jumping on the goal post and tearing it down?

A. Rick Dickson, Dick Rickson, or Dick Nixon.

Q. Now that "To Tell the Truth" is back on the air, will the real Tulane AD please stand up?

A. Gone but not forgotten, forgotten but not gone.

Q. What's the difference between Bear Bryant and Joe Dean?

A. Somebody lost the six-pack.

Q. Why did Tulane cancel its pre-game tailgating party?

A. He was trying to count to 21.

Q. Why was the Tiger player arrested for indecent exposure?

A. A digital clock, a Metairie parade and Tulane football.

Q. Name something with no hands, no bands and no fans.

A. "I don't own a pornograph."

Q. What did the Tiger fan say when he was charged with selling pornography in Broussard Hall?

A. Because everybody had to take two.

Q. Why did Tulane stop giving "Greenie Babies" to the first 5,000 people at the game?

A. The Electoral College.

Q. Who did Joe Dean try to schedule for LSU's homecoming game?

A. **Same number of musicians.**

Q. What do the Tulane band and the Dixie Chicks have in common?

A. **The job description calls for experience in the criminal justice system.**

Q. Why does LSU want DA Doug Moreau to become AD Doug Moreau?

A. **Guatemala, Panama, Grenada and Tulane.**

Q. Name four victories that took Army about three hours.

A. **Who wants to be a millionaire?**

Q. What was LSU's recruiting pitch to hire Nick Saban?

A. **27,342.**

Q. By Tulane's count, how many people were on the initial "Survivor" show?

A. **Dillard's, Jim Morrison, Mewelde, the Democratic candidate and Joe Dean.**

Q. Name a store, a Door, a Moore, a Gore and a bore.

A. **A Mormon school in Utah and the Tulane football team.**

Q. Name two athletic programs always referred to as "Young."

A. **A .500 record in CUSA.**

Q. What does LSU have that it doesn't want and Tulane wants that it doesn't have?

A. **Undergrad school.**

Q. What do you call the best six years of a Tiger student's life?

A. **Don't ask/Don't tell.**

Q. What is the Army's policy on gays and what was the Army-Tulane final score?

A. **Rudolph, a mother hen and Joe Dean.**

Q. Name a famous buck, a dame cluck and a lame duck.

A. **The networks' predictions about the Florida vote.**

Q. Name the only people that blew more calls than CUSA officials this year.

A. **Abdul D. Tentmakur, Tommy Bowden and Mack Brown.**

Q. Name three of the world's most famous nomads.

A. He saw 911 on the side and thought it was a Porsche.
Q. Why did the Tiger linebacker steal a police car?
A. Because it made him more obscure than being in the
Federal Witness Relocation Program.
Q. Why did the Mafia informant become a Tulane season
ticket holder?
A. Harrah's Casino, Jazzland and the Booty brothers.
Q. Name three groups that haven't produced in Louisiana as
advertised.
A. Jimmy Hoffa's whereabouts, Nicole Brown Simpson's
murderer and Tulane's pass coverage.
Q. What has remained undiscovered for years?
A. Faulty sex education.
Q. Why does LSU put Vaseline on its goalposts?
A. Tulane at LSU on Sept. 1.
Q. How does the 2001 football season open?

Abdul D. Tentmakur

October 29, 2000

Through the years frustrated Saints fans calling in to Buddy
Diliberto's post-game talk show on WWL radio have included such
luminaries as Sid in Jefferson, Bubba on His Magic Carpet, Dr.
Kevorkian, The Inquisitor, Sandman and Whistle Monster.

But one of Buddy D's legendary pack of "squirrels," as the
Master of Dilibonics refers to some of those who dial in to "The
Point After" and predict the Saints are going to the Super Bowl after
a two-point win over Atlanta, may be beginning to distance himself
from the pack.

If Buddy D, the fearless slayer of the English language, is indeed
the Amir of the Airwaves, the Rajah of the Radio, then Abdul D.
Tentmakur has climbed to the top of the mountain of those calling
in every Sunday during the season.

For the past few weeks, Abdul has not only been calling in, commenting on the game in his Bedouin-esque accent, he's been singing song parodies he's composed about his Saints and playing his guitar on the air. Last Sunday he unveiled his latest effort, "Bad Bad L'Roi Glover," sung to the tune of "Bad Bad Leroy Brown."

"On the south side of New Orleans, in the football side of town,
"There is a brother name of L'roi Glover, who loves knocking
people down.
"You see L'roi is a tackle, and he stands about 6 foot 2,
"And if you try to pass he's gonna kick your ass, and hand it back
to you."
Chorus:
"Cause he's Bad Bad L'roi Glover. He's one quarterback sackin'
mother.
"Yeah, he's meaner than a junkyard dog and he loves when the blitz
is on."

Speaking this week from one of his nomadic watering holes, Sidney's Sports Bar on Barataria Boulevard in Marrero, "Abdul" joked that he lives on the side of a mountain in what he describes as "a humongous tent," and that when he is out tending his sheep and goats in a valley below, "Ze songs, zey come to me."

It's the sort of broad, stereotypical comedy that's bound to offend some Arab-Americans – but then listening to Buddy D's show has never been a good idea for the easily offended or politically correct.

Abdul D. Tentmakur is the alter ego of Al d'Aquin, a 38-year-old offshore pipeline worker who was a class clown at Archbishop Shaw High School. D'Aquin is a husband and father of two kids, a coach and parent at PARD Playground, the president of the Visitation of Our Lady School Co-Op (PTA), a baseball umpire, a huge Tulane football fan, a golfer and a big-time outdoorsman who travels to Colorado and other states to hunt deer.

Not exactly a squirrel. As he says, "Not a lot of grass grows under my feet."

Abdul was born some years ago during the Jim Mora era when the Saints started off 5-0 and fans started slamming Buddy because he wouldn't climb on the bandwagon. Buddy allowed that if the Saints got to the Super Bowl he'd wear a dress to the game but he was so large he'd probably have to have a tentmaker make it for him.

"I had had a few beers and my brother got after me to call in, so I did," said d'Aquin. "It was the first time. I had never called into a radio station in my life. I don't know where the voice came from – it just happened."

He does other accents, too. "I got into 'Braveheart' a few years back and for a while I talked like Mel Gibson."

The year that started out 5-0 collapsed, of course. The Saints started losing.

"I was calling in, giving updates on making the dress, saying I had my wives working on it, and Buddy D was asking me: 'So now that the Saints have gone in the tank, what are you going to do with that dress?' (I told him) A friend of mine's daughter was getting married and I told him I'd give it to her."

"She must be huge," said Diliberto.

"No" Abdul shot back, "zey're going to leeve een eet."

"I got him pretty good with that one," said d'Aquin. "I think we hit it off pretty good after that."

"He's sharp," said Diliberto.

During the week, when he is driving to Venice (the one in Louisiana, not Italy) in his truck, d'Aquin composes his song parodies and regularly breaks into character.

"I start doing the voice so I keep it fresh and good," he said. "The toughest thing is singing in character – it's hard to do."

D'Aquin played bass guitar in high school, was in a couple of bands. "But you can't sit around campfires playing bass, so I took some guitar lessons."

Each Carnival season, Al/Abdul dons another hat — he and a few other musicians become "The Memory Makers" and ride and play in several parades including Thoth, Cleopatra and Argus.

"Buddy's show has a life of its own," he said. "I listen to it not just because I call in but because it's funny. All those people driving home to outlying cities — that's what makes it work."

D'Aquin's family — wife Kim, daughter Ashley, son Scott – and some friends know he is Abdul.

"The offshore guys know it and ask me how I think the Saints are going to do each week like I have a pipeline to the team," he said. "The only thing I know is that it's a lot easier to come up with material when they're winning."

Mrs. Tentmakur, he said, loves the comments about Abdul paying off his bets in wives and sheep, "as long as I don't lose her to Akeem the bookie and maintain one wife." She even made him a costume, a black robe and turban with gold fleurs-de-lis which he wears – only occasionally – to the games. Since he is hunting and camping a lot during the season, he goes to only about three or four.

"When people recognize me as Abdul, it kind of strokes me a little. They've put me up on the big screen a couple of times. That's fun. Signing autographs is fun. I walk into Hardhead's bar on the way to Lafitte and they shout, 'Abdul!' That's neat. I always stay optimistic, but I don't get on those 10-6 bandwagons. Deep down in my black and gold heart, however, I still think we can beat St. Louis."

After the game against Arizona today, listen for Abdul's call. As most folks know, the Saints are looking for a name for their top-ranked defense and fans have been calling in with suggestions, a lot of them pretty lame. Abdul is leaning toward "Swamp Dogs" and today you just might hear this ditty, possibly to the tune of "Marie Laveau":

"Down in Louisiana where the Saints call home
There's a pack of dogs inside the Superdome
They play football and they play it well
They're the best damn defense in the NFL
They're the Dogs! Ruffff! The Swamp Dogs!"

Chorus:
"Well, they're half pit bull and half alligator
They're a mean ass bunch of quarterback haters
So if you don't want your quarterback sacked again
You better punt the ball on first and 10.
Against the Dogs! Ruffff! The Swamp Dogs!"

And obviously, what will follow is the Baha Men with: *"Who let the dogs out? Ruffff! Ruffff!"*

CHAPTER 8
The Parade's Comin'

Carnival's Supersleuth: Deep Float

January 31, 2001

The worn black trenchcoat, stubble beard, fake moustache, sunglasses and hat pulled down low may have been a disguise that works for most people but when I spotted this familiar personage late at night last week, I knew it was my legendary contact.

"I have emerged. I am on duty," said Deep Float in his raspy voice. "We've expanded the operation. No one will escape us."

Float, the most famous covert Carnival double secret agent in history, stood at the end of the bar looking as disheveled as ever, but eager to get to work. He handed me a piece of paper, which turned out to be his business card. It said:

"Tuned in to the new millennium: We are 2001 compatible and politically corrupt. DEEP FLOAT. Covert Carnival Espionage specializing in: Leaks to the media. Theft of mystic secrets. Unmasking of royalty. Dial 1-800-COVER-UP. New services: Character assassinations. King cake baby abductions. Black market beads. Floatjacking."

"Impressive," I told him. "I always knew you could pick up where Inspector Clouseau left off and take it a notch further."

"I resemble that remark," he snapped. "I am not a bungler like Clouseau. My reputation is impeccable. I am Deep Float: supersleuth. Never forget it. Your Mardi Gras stuff dies without me. No one can get into dens like I can. No one but Deep Float can penetrate the impenetrable. My X-ray X-rated Covert-O-Camera is now digital. Comus, Momus – I go through the thickest walls and find out anything you want to know about their parades."

"That would be useful. Lemme know what you find since they don't parade anymore," I informed him.

"Okay, wise guy. You know what I mean. Any parade — Proteus, Rex, d'Etat, Chaos, Druids, how's that?"

"Let's do it. We make a great team and I make you sound intelligent. It's only 17 days till the first parade and time to get to work. So where have you been all these months, reinventing mule-drawn floats?"

"Actually, I was in Florida for some time observing the presidential recount. Ballot box manipulation is something Deep Float Inc. might add to its services. Then, of course, I've been re-establishing contacts."

"You mean you were rounding up Float's flotilla of feckless reckless spies? You must have found some good bail bondsmen."

"Actually, I was consulting with such intermediaries as Sarcophagus I, Quasimodo the Humpteenth and the exiled former king of Le Gran Cru de Mentia, all trusted operatives. But the rest of the year I was, ahem, deep into researching Mardi Gras history. It's absolutely fascinating."

"What did you find?"

"Well, one thing that intrigued me was how the colors of Carnival were selected in 1872 by the King of Carnival. Now everybody thinks purple was chosen for justice, green for faith and gold for power, right?"

"That's what I've always heard."

"Well, I found that purple and gold were chosen for Louisiana State University and green for Tulane. I can understand the Tulane part anyway. Who has to keep the faith more than Tulane fans?"

"Good point. And I guess you're going to tell me LSU has the power, but where does justice come in?"

"I'm working on that. Criminal justice, maybe?"

"In 1872? I doubt it."

"Well, it's a work in progress. Here's something interesting. Most krewes have kings or queens. D'Etat has a Dictator, which is different and there is no queen, no court and no ball – the Dictator did away with it all. But Babylon, if you've ever seen them, has a Sargon."

"And?"

"Well, Sargon about 4,500 years ago was a king of Babylon, a city known for its luxury and immorality where the famous Hanging Gardens, one of the Seven Wonders of the World, were located. Are you impressed with this research or what?"

"Or what."

"Well, then you might want to know that Babylon is half the answer to a meteorological question about Mardi Gras. Only two parades in Carnival history have been snowed out. One was Babylon in 1958, which kept the Sargon hunkered down in his den, and the other was Proteus in 1899. Babylon wound up sneaking into the Saturday parade schedule, but Proteus did something absolutely weird, if my research is correct."

"And what would that be?"

"They paraded on the Friday after Mardi Gras, during Lent."

"Hard to believe."

"Well, believe it. Remember who dug this up – the greatest — me, the one, the only, Deep Float."

"Exactly my point. I rest my case."

No Pain, No Gain: Mardi Gras Fitness Training

February 23, 2003

Mardi Gras Marathon Weekend – the glut of parades and partying that lasts from Friday night through Tuesday, not the 26-mile race – is only five days away.

Here are some general tips to get you in shape to survive this Bacchanalian orgy and a day-by-day guide to the next week of training. Remember to wake up before starting your workout.

If you've been counting calories, eating healthy and dieting, it's time to give that lifestyle a rest. You've got to get in shape – and quickly! You can't go into this weekend of debauchery without raising your tolerance levels.

Fish and chicken, vegetables, fresh fruit and fiber may serve you fine the other weeks of the year – but it won't get you through this ordeal. You need different food groups.

Here's a five-day fitness crash course for both parents and non-parents. The diet is the same for both.

SUNDAY:

Breakfast: Extra spicy Bloody Mary, no celery, two large slices of king cake, preferably stuffed with cream cheese, four slices bacon. Lunch: Six deviled eggs, half jar pickled okra, dozen finger sandwiches, bag of Zapp's Crawgator potato chips. Afternoon snack: Chocolate covered pecans. Dinner: Cheese and crackers, unlimited Buffalo wings and drumettes, jambalaya, two to four beers.

Exercise: Parents: Walk a half mile carrying four folding chairs and a ladder. Non-parents: Walk to the nearest convenience store, buy four bags of ice, a case of drinks and a case of beer and carry it all home.

MONDAY:

Breakfast: Large milk punch, three large slices of cinnamon pecan king cake, Egg McMuffin with cheese. Lunch: Oyster po-boy, fries, two beers. Afternoon snack: Unlimited salted peanuts. Dinner: Strawberry daiquiri, fried chicken and biscuits and red beans from Popeyes.

Exercise: Parents: Stand on a ladder for two hours. Non-parents: Run alongside a moving vehicle for two blocks yelling and waving your hands.

TUESDAY:

Breakfast: Large screwdriver, half a king cake, corn dog on a stick. Lunch: Whole muffaletta, four beers. Afternoon snack: cotton candy, bag of buttered popcorn. Dinner: Garlic breadsticks with cheese dip, extra large pepperoni and sausage pizza with green peppers and onions, two bottles cheap red wine.

Exercise: Parents: Raise your pain threshold. Stand up for four hours, drink three gallons of water but don't go to the potty. Non-parents: Play "Mardi Gras Mambo" on your stereo 20 straight times and dance until after midnight.

WEDNESDAY:

Breakfast: Milk punch and Bloody Mary. Dozen Krispy Kreme doughnuts or half king cake, double filled with your choice of fillings. Leftover cold pizza. Lunch: Two hot dogs (preferably Lucky Dogs) with mustard, chili, cheese, onions, jalapenos, large bag Crawgator chips, four Turbodogs. Afternoon snack: Five pounds boiled crawfish. Dinner: Frozen top shelf margaritas, unlimited chips and salsa, guacamole, 4-6 tacos, dozen Manuel's hot tamales.

Exercise: Parents: Fill four plastic bags with leftover beads until they each weigh ten pounds. Walk a brisk mile with them without resting. Non-parents: Go to a nightclub and dance every dance. Do not come home until daylight.

THURSDAY:

Breakfast: Jello shots, leftover tamales, leftover pizza with imprint of face in it, leftover stale king cake. Lunch: Roast beef po-boy, dressed, extra mayo, cheese fries, four draft beers in frozen mugs. Afternoon snack: Fried Popeyes chicken livers and bag of Cheetos. Dinner: Mini-muffalettas, spicy Cajun dip, baked brie, spinach and artichoke dip, party meatballs, cheese fondue with French bread, assorted other hors d'oeuvres. Salad optional, unlimited beer or wine.

Exercise: Parents: Put a ladder in your back yard and stay up all night and guard it. Non-parents: Load a large cooler with drinks and ice and carry it for 12-16 blocks without taking a break. Or, get a neighbor to park your car about 10 blocks in any direction from your house and then try to find it.

FRIDAY:

Breakfast: At Brennan's. Lunch: At Galatoire's. Afternoon snack: At the Old Absinthe House. Dinner: Go straight to the starting line on a neutral ground near you and wait for the Krewe of Hermes and Le Krewe d'Etat. Bring well-stocked cooler, backup cooler, 24-piece box of Popeyes, ham and swiss po-boys, two dozen brownies, your cell phone and a roll of duct tape. Hold that position for 96 hours.

Sleep optional. If you followed the training guide, you're now in top condition. Good luck with the marathon.

Trow Me Sumthin', Mistuh!

February 25, 2001

By any standards, New Orleans is a difficult city to get a handle on if you're here for a long weekend. Even if you live here and it's a normal weekend, you sometimes say to yourself: Go figure.

But this weekend is light years from normal in a city inhabited by countless professional party animals who dedicate their lives to hedonism. Normal for them is already "pretty out there." Well, this is the weekend they head for another galaxy and take a step up on the Revelry Richter Scale.

Since Friday, we have been in the midst of the wackiest, wildest five-day weekend of the year — when altered states of consciousness are the norm, not the exception. Maskers on floats seem to ride through every street you want to cross, tossing worthless but much-cherished beads and other throws to onlookers. If the weather's good, the city's outside, dining and drinking al fresco, just hanging out, waiting for the next parade.

These onlookers, these trained observers of Carnival past and present — many of them costumed themselves — will go to the mat and fight each other for such baubles as talking beanie bears, blinking beads, squirting toilet seats, rubber chickens, plastic cups, flying discs, coconuts and stuffed animals that will wind up in attics on Ash Wednesday with a collective worth of zilch.

And these locals will speak a tongue – frequently in tongues – that will be Yat (New Orleans for Greek) to the outsider.

Insider N'Awlins language is difficult to translate. Insider N'Awlins Carnival jargon is all but impossible. Throw, er, trow in the occasionally incomprehensible dialect dat is spoken here by many of da denizens, and what we could easily have is communication gridlock. Here, for puzzled first-time visitors, courtesy of the Cliché College of Carnival Knowledge (not a subsidiary of the University of Phoenix) is some of His Royal Lardship's Royal Lexicon, the 2001 edition.

139

Gross: Sure, some of what you see in the French Quarter might be, depending on your sensitivities. But gross at Carnival means how much a rider throws, er, trows. One who likes to trow a decent amount will carry 30 gross of beads. Some maskers on Thoth, a krewe known for its generosity that parades Uptown today, have been known to toss anywhere from 60-100 gross of beads on their lengthy route.

Campas: What a lot of people park near da route for da parish parades and what you see none of in da city. These party headquarters offer R&R from the firing line of the route, bladder relief and refreshments. Most folks call 'em RVs. Don't say camp-ers. We won't understand. It's campas, accent on the cam.

Ettes: That's "ettes" as in Ursulettes, Carmelettes. Eaglettes, Pistolettes, Drumettes, whatever-ettes they are. These synchronized girl groups dance the dance, walk the walk, talk the talk. They kick, they march, they tap, they click, they strut, they twirl their batons, they shake their pom-poms, they do their thing. If you're lucky, they do it with a band. If not, get ready for an auditory attack from a boom box on top of a truck. Note to parade-goers: The Carmelettes should not be confused with the Carmelites, an order of nuns not known for this sort of activity. Applaud when the various ettes go by. They're young and they work hard at this.

Gras: Just like there's a lot of fat in good berled crabs, there's a lot of Gras in Carnival these days. Used to be there was only Mardi Gras, Fat Tuesday and the Boeuf Gras (Fatted Calf) float in Rex. But now there is the Lundi Gras celebration on Fat Monday and Le Krewe d'Etat celebrates Vendredi Gras, Fat Friday. Samedi Gras, Fat Saturday, and Dimanche Gras, Fat Sunday, would seem to be in order since New Orleans is annually rated high on the fattest-cities-in-the-country listings.

Doubloon: Formerly a Spanish gold coin romanticized in pirate movies, individual krewe doubloons are now endangered throws. Once very popular, they were done in by mass overproduction causing the bottom to fall out of the doubloon collecting market. Riders don't want to throw them because parade-goers don't try to catch them.

Trow: Mentioned earlier, trow is either a noun or a verb. A rider on a float trows trows. The noun "trow" means something trown, such as beads or panties. The voib "trow" means to toss or fling something so that it becomes airborne after being propelled, hopefully toward a parade-goer who will have earlier yelled, "Trow me sumthin', mistuh!" This is not that complicated but catching trows is a true art form involving coordination and dexterity. It is perfected by many locals whose considerable talents are frequently impaired by consumption of adult beverages.

Yat: Not a seasonal Carnival term at all, but a year-round one, "Yat" has become a term of endearment for certain residents of the city who have not mastered the King's English, which is understandable because no one here has. There's a little Yat in all natives. For visitors only: Yats are called Yats because they say, "Where y'at?" That is a greeting which has nothing to do with physical location and loosely translates as, "How's it goin'?" Trust me.

Route, as in parade route: Poe-tate-oh, poe-tot-oh. Toe-mate-oh, toe-mot-oh. Parade rout or parade root. Whatever your pro-nun-see-a-shun, see ya dere on da route. And Happy Mardi Gras!

CHAPTER 9

Railbirds and Rogues

Richie Della the Paper Seller

February 2, 1980

The first day you knew for sure that he wasn't going to be back in the Richards Building selling newspapers was the kind of day that no racehorse handicapper in the world – not even Richie Della – liked to fool with.

Outside the overheated lobby, rain poured down through the gloom onto Gravier Street. Two people across from the newsstand ran into the Commercial Restaurant, and one of them slipped as he got to the door. A car stopped in front of the Commerce Garage and the guy behind him hit his brakes, skidding to a near miss.

It was Tuesday afternoon. If they had been running at the Fair Grounds that day, the tote board would have shown the track conditions as "sloppy." By the 10th race, it would have been so dark the track announcer would have his problems seeing the backside. "M'boy, ya can't figure nuthin' in this weather," Richie Della would say. "You can find a horse dat likes da mud, but how ya know he likes da rain?"

A pickup truck pulled up and dumped four bundles of newspapers on the sidewalk. Frank Cullins picked them up and brought them inside the double doors. He stacked them neatly on top of a folding stool next to a marble wall. He moved a small dark blue coin box and began cutting open the bundles.

Josie Winter, an elevator starter for 30 years, spoke up. "Frank, you lost your little buddy last night, huh?"

"Yeah, Richie . . . that's sumthin', huh?" he replied while he continued to sort his papers. "I known Richie 50 years. We both sold papers back in the old days, back when you had to fight for a corner. Those days are gone, though . . . I been selling since I was 9 . . . guess he probably sold that long, too. How old was he?"

"Seventy," was the answer.

"Yeah, well I'm 69," said Cullins. "I guess that's about right. There ain't many of us left. And poor Johnny Schuermann, we lost that boy in January." (That "boy" was 80 years old, and had sold papers at Camp and Canal for 62 years.)

Sure, Anthony J. Richidella, the fella the people downtown knew as "Richie Della the Paper Seller," hadn't been at his stand since early in January when he got bad news from the doctor. But nothing's ever over 'til it's over, right? And since Richie – the guy racetrackers knew as the handicapper "Speed Form" – had been bucking odds his whole life, well, there was always a hope. He was still coming downtown to say hello to his friends. Longshots gotta win some of the time, right?

When Richie gave up selling, Cullins, who had already retired, came back to help him out. No rookie himself, Cullins peddled papers for 27 years at the NBC building on Baronne and later was a night wholesaler for 16 years. "I just took this to get out of the house, but I don't see how Richie was making anything on it," he said.

The answer is: He wasn't. At $3.35 a hundred and selling about four bundles a day, it didn't take a brain as sharp as Richie's to figure out he didn't do it for money. So why? The answer to that isn't so tough, either: Both his brothers were newsboys, the people down there were his family; and he just couldn't leave – he had been down on the farm too long.

"I'm convinced he knew 90 percent of the people in New Orleans," Cullins said. "He knew the bigshots and the little guys. He always had a good word for them and everybody had a good word for him." At Richie's funeral yesterday, there was a wreath from the brake tag station. A lot of people said that would give you a good idea of how many friends he had. He never owned a car.

"M'boy, it don't cost nuthin' to say thank you," Richie liked to say.

But what he knew best was racehorses, and there were plenty of reasons for it. Almost every morning, he ate sunrise breakfast at the A&G cafeteria at Canal and Broad with some mutuel clerks who were his friends. If he wasn't talking about horses there, it was at the Hummingbird Grill or the pancake shop.

They would review yesterday's races, complain about bad rides, and pore over The Daily Racing Form. Then he would come into the office and he and veteran States-Item handicapper Pete Hearty would do the same thing. "The funny thing about Richie," Pete was saying, "is that he always claimed to be one of the $2 bettors, but he'd think nothing of making a $40 show parlay. All that stuff about the tailor-made shirts, imported cigars and alligator shoes – it's all true."

"M'boy, for 10 percent more, you can always go first class," Richie said.

Hearty says Richie was so well-liked because he'd do anything in the world for people. "He knew Red Smith well, and there's a reason for that, too. He gave Red a couple of live horses once, and Red always looked for him at the Derby after that."

Having a lot of friends who played the horses, Richie would always get calls at the newspaper from people who wanted to find out how their horse ran. Since it is against rules to give race results over the phone, Richie had a unique way of handling their requests.

"The mailman brought that package and it cost $7.80," Richie would say. That was good news. The bad news was either "The undertaker got him" or "The groceries are gonna cost you $10."

Richie didn't know it, but he was going to be inducted into the Fair Grounds Press Box Hall of Fame this Valentine's Day. Eddie Arcaro was going to fly in for the occasion, which might have brought on one of the few times you would have caught Richie speechless.

Richie lived to do favors for people, like getting them tickets to the Sugar Bowl or hotel reservations. One of the reservations he had made recently was for himself, for the first week of May in

Louisville. He had asked the doctor if he could hear "My Old Kentucky Home" one more time, and the doc had given him the go-ahead to make the reservations.

Seeing Richie in the pressbox at Churchill Downs, rolling his cigar back and forth in his mouth, was a delight. He was a hog in slop, Br'er Rabbit in the briar patch. Not seeing him will be a different story.

One thing's not gonna happen here, though. No sloppy endings. Richie was a dry wit – the master of the one-liner – and he wouldn't want it that way. Not somebody who once stole a page from Yogi Berra when he said, "Nobody ever goes down to the French Quarter anymore – it's too crowded."

Or the day Richie was hawking papers outside the door on Gravier Street, yelling, "Heyyyy! Fiiii-nullll! Last edition! Final race results!" and this priest walks by.

"Son," said the priest, "I walk by here every day and all I ever hear you yell is race results, race results. Isn't there anything else besides race results in that paper?"

"Yes, sir," said Richie. "We got tomorrow's entries inside."

Hard Times and the Horses

November 29, 1975

"You can beat a race but you can't beat the races" is the motto that carried "Hard Times" Vince through the best of times and the worst of times.

At 67, the legendary Irish Channel handicapper is as much a fixture as the finish line – tattered and wrinkled, sometimes tapped out – but living proof of bucking the system for more than half a century and avoiding a 9-to-5 job.

"A professional turf advisor – not a tout," as he described himself, Earl Vince was once a promising young jockey from First and Chippewa streets. A broken leg and subsequent weight problem

145

turned him to training thoroughbreds, and one of his charges even chased the great Coaltown around racetracks in 1948.

Those were the best of times.

Through it all, Hard Times watched horses run and he learned how to bet. Undaunted by bad judgments, the Depression, enough losing tickets to stuff a horse, and luck that would send many people to the bridge, he survived. If nothing more, he is a monument to persistence and the belief that a little good handicapping, from time to time, can keep anybody out of the chair of despair.

When the Fair Grounds opened its doors last Friday, there was the ever-present figure of Hard Times – slightly disheveled, short a couple of days' shaves, his furrowed brow frowning at an uncooperative oddsboard as he shuffled around the grandstand, not making anybody a believer of his claims he is losing his zest for racing.

"He was there when they sprung the latch for race number one," says a cohort. "And he'll be there till the bugler blows 'Taps' for him."

Sometime during the '30s, Vince had some of his worst of times. He was training horses at Aurora Downs outside of Chicago and felt sorry for a young rider who wasn't getting too many mounts named Johnny Longden.

Longden rode for Hard Times that day, and when the horse came back a well-beaten fifth, Vince was beside himself. "Jock, you better get in some other business before you get killed," he shouted angrily as Longden dismounted.

"You swung to hit the horse, missed the horse, threw the whip away, and almost fell off. You sure can't ride."

Despite Vince's evaluation of his talent, Longden kept riding. In 1966, after 40 years in the saddle, Johnny Longden retired after winning the 6,026th race of his storied career, during which time the horses he rode earned $24.7 million. He is generally regarded as one of the greatest riders of all time, and capped his career by winning the rich San Juan Capistrano Handicap on a horse named George Royal – the very last horse he would ever ride.

How did Hard Times miss? "I'd have laid 20 million to one he'da never made it," Times recalled of his mistaken judgment. "He was the worst I ever seen. He was lucky to come back alive. I never seen anybody look so bad on a horse's back."

Although history proved him dead wrong, Vince says it was Longden's guts that made him great. "Any other jock woulda quit. The kid had absolutely no promise – you'da never think he'd become a jockey."

Things were tough all over during those times, and recovery from the Depression, even for racetrackers like Hard Times, was based on so-called sound judgments and speculation in "sure things," not necessarily meaning 8-to-5 shots.

The winters of distress that followed Black Friday, 1929, did not spare the hardboot gypsies who ventured south each year to Col. E.R. Bradley's Gentilly oval. Behind the track on Belfort Street, in places like Red Stokes' bar, grooms split cans of beer and cigarettes, huddled outside around fires built in trashcans, halved weenies for dinner and made two-bit show parlays.

Things weren't any better on the other side of the track, money was tight, high rollers were scarce and the golden Bradley days were coming to a close. The colonel retired to his beloved Idle Hour farm in Kentucky and by Feb. 1 of 1933, purses at the track were down to $500.

The nation was in a crisis state when President Roosevelt took office in March of 1933. Panic-stricken depositors had made runs on banks that made last-second dashes to daily double windows look like kiddy-corner stuff. More than $1.5 billion was lifted by people running scared.

Roosevelt closed the nation's banks almost immediately, forcing the Fair Grounds to padlock its turnstile for a while, cash being a necessity. Things were at their blackest then and not even the most brazen bookie would lay odds on the future of the track. "I'll never forget them days," said Vince.

In this bleakest of settings, Roosevelt tried to dispel fears: "This great nation will endure as it has endured, will revive and will prosper," he guaranteed them. "So first of all, let me assert my firm belief that the only thing we have to fear is fear itself."

Somewhere out there, Hard Times was listening. He got

Roosevelt's message about fear and endurance loud and clear – because his path was never to be lined with flowers or riches and he would never fear the most ominous omens.

An example:

Last year during the transit strike, as is his custom, Hard Times was catching a ride to the track. He was in more than his usual hurry because he had a move on the daily double.

He hitched a ride with a truck on St. Charles Avenue and two blocks on the other side of Canal, the truck had a flat. Vince got out, spotted a friend, and got a ride with him to Esplanade where the car conked out.

Frantic, Hard Times stuck out his thumb again, caught his third ride of the day, only to have the driver pulled over by police, and ticketed and arrested for driving without a license.

He finally called a cab in desperation, got to the track in time to bet and see his horse run, as they say on the backside, "absolutely."

"Two or three breakdowns, I shoulda gone home, turned around. That was nuthin' but bad luck," he remembered. Later that day, Times finally bet on a winner but the horse was disqualified, and he was blanked for the day. But not discouraged. "There's no such thing as superstition or bad luck," he said.

Indefatigable – that's the word.

Despite himself, some of Hard Times' betting theories were sound. He never bet every race, which is the sure sign of a big loser, but picked his spots, often going for weeks without wagering.

He doesn't read the Daily Racing Form at all, explaining, "The Form just tells you what a horse did last week" — preferring to watch a horse two or three times through his high-powered binoculars before he bets – when he thinks the horse is ready to win.

Hard Times would walk across the track every day, not because of any superstition, but to get a feel for what he considered a "tricky track," knowing that track surfaces change daily and certain horses prefer different types of tracks – fast, wet fast, muddy, deep, holding, cuppy, etc.

"But it's like any athletic sport," he believed. "Ninety percent of this business is condition. A $5,000 horse can beat a $10,000 horse if he's right. That's what I base my gambling on – condition over class.

"I rode 'em and I know 'em. If a horse drifts out, he's getting tired and his legs are hurting. Men who are supposed to be experts blame their riders for that. That just proves they don't know anything."

Every time Vince spots something unusual, he has a big book at home in which he logs his comments on the day's races – bad ride, bad left knee, drifted out, swollen ankle, sore in left front.

"Nobody can beat the races," he said. "But when I bet, you can bet that little horsie is going to be runnin'."

When he thinks he's ready to make a kill, he still doesn't like to spread the word around, not even tout his friends. "If I lose my money, I don't give a damn. But I hate to see another guy lose his money."

Everybody at the Fair Grounds knows Hard Times — but Earl Vince is a no-name.

"He just looks like hard times," said a regular. "He's been down so long he thinks he's up."

"He got his name during the Depression," said another, just one of the stories about how Vince got his moniker that are all wrong.

"I was boxing for Kingsley House, bantamweight about 118 pounds," he recalled. "I was fightin' this guy and he was gettin' to me pretty good. Sam Pizzitola was in my corner. I come back to the corner between rounds and Sam asks, 'How ya doin', kid?'

"I'm having hard times," Vince said. They never left him.

Frankie Struck It Rich

April 14, 2009

The big score.

For every hustler, gambler, card shark, racetracker and lottery player, it's the never-ending dream – the day your ship comes in, the pot of gold at the end of the rainbow, the day you ride off into the sunset, top-down on your new convertible.

Or take your newfound wealth and . . . buy a bar?

Meet Frankie Mazzanti, a native of Lake Village, Arkansas, who spent his formative years splitting his time driving to Oaklawn Park Racetrack in Hot Springs and Louisiana Downs in Bossier City – matriculating in the Investment College of Racehorse Knowledge.

Mazzanti, a large, friendly man and self-described "country boy," was sitting at a table in the back of his neighborhood bar, 45 Tchoup, near Tipitina's on Tchoupitoulas Street, spinning his version of the oft-told tale about coming to New Orleans and never leaving.

"I was betting more and enjoying it less, so I trimmed back," he said of his earlier financial career. Then in 1998, his brother, an engineer in New Orleans, was going to Thailand for a job and asked Frankie to watch his apartment. Hmmm. The French Quarter, the Fair Grounds Race Course, the food, the music – it wasn't a tough decision. He got a job tending bar in the Quarter and eventually met Jeff Carreras, the owner of Parasol's.

"Nine years of steady, or unsteady employment," he said. He befriended another Parasol's bartender, Debbie Shatz, and they talked about perhaps one day buying Parasol's since Carreras was considering bailing out and moving to California.

Then Katrina hit. Parasol's was one of those bars that remained high and dry. "His business went through the roof and he decided not to leave," said Mazzanti.

After working the late shift on Friday, May 5, 2006, he had to go make Derby bets for about 40 different Parasol's customers on

Saturday at the Gretna OTB parlor. "I almost overslept," he admitted. He also had to make his own bets, which included a lot of $1 trifectas and $1 superfectas. (In a trifecta, horses have to finish in a 1-2-3 order and in a superfecta 1-2-3-4.) Mazzanti is especially fond of superfectas for a couple of reasons.

"I like to scattershot the Derby. I play a whole lot of superfectas. There's no other race of the year where there are 20 horses, 20 different betting propositions and the whole country is betting. It's almost like a little lottery," he said. Like many handicappers, he is attracted to longshots. "It can happen anytime, anywhere – all I need is to see a horse that showed a little spark."

Mazzanti had spent days devouring the Daily Racing Form for the 132nd Derby, which wound up being won by the ill-fated Barbaro. He studied track bias that day, whether the racing surface was playing to speed horses or closers. And he particularly zeroed in on a horse named Bluegrass Cat, who had been one of the top three-year-olds that year, until he ran a clunker in the Blue Grass Stakes at Keeneland.

"I just threw out his last race," he said. "You can always figure out a reason to throw out a race. At Keeneland that year, horses that weren't within three lengths of the lead at the top of the stretch couldn't win. He wasn't and he didn't. But he was the one I thought would win the Derby."

He didn't do that either, but he ran second at odds of 30-1. Third was the oddly-named Steppenwolfer, at 16-1 ridden by local favorite Robby Albarado. Fourth place was a dead heat, between Brother Derek (almost 8-1) and Jazil (24-1). Winner Barbaro went off at 6-1.

It had taken him a while to make the bets, and when he got back home he dozed off. He got a call from Parasol's asking him if had seen the race. "I turned it on, it was just over, but I saw the replay.

"It took a minute, but I was in shock. I'm still in shock. It was outrageous," he said. He had bet, he said, between $140-$160 on the race. His $5 exacta paid almost $1,470. His $1 trifecta paid over $5,700. And his $1 superfecta, which included Jazil, paid $42,430.

"At a different point in my life I might have done what some

151

handicappers do when they hit the big one – go to Florida in the winter, spend summers at Saratoga in New York, take a year off and see if I could make it as a professional handicapper," he said. But he was pushing 50. "I had even thought about going back to college. "But I had done that for six years and I was still a junior."

Instead, he got Debbie Shatz to partner with him and they went hunting for a bar in the Uptown area. "We got lucky with this place," he said of 45 Tchoup. "Good timing, it was high and dry, we gutted it. Debbie's husband is a woodworker and everything you see in here is all from salvaged wood."

It's a typical neighborhood bar with regulars – but 45 Tchoup also gets a before and after crowd from Tipitina's and nearby Dick & Jenny's restaurant. In front hang the flags of three teams, once the trifecta of losers: the Saints, the Red Sox and the Cubs.

"This (the bar) was the only way this was going to happen," he said of his big score. "People ask me all the time when they find out, are you way ahead? And I say, no, no way. I've been betting for 30 years, and the money I gambled over all those years, I just got it all back at one time."

As for this year's Derby, he said of the race he's never seen in person, "People ask me who I like. I don't know. I hate to steer anybody wrong."

Back in the Saddle:
The Lamarque & Roussel Road Show

May 1, 2008

Twenty years ago, the Ronnie Lamarque Triple Crown road show with Risen Star wowed 'em in Louisville, Baltimore and New York City.

Long before blaring out "Volare!" at the end of one of his colorful Lamarque Ford TV commercials, the flamboyant car salesman sang his way to two-thirds of thoroughbred racing's golden trifecta — the Preakness Stakes and Belmont Stakes — in 1988. That was the year that Star captured the Preakness and the Belmont after getting into traffic and running third in the Derby.

Lamarque's crowning moment came at Pimlico Race Course when ABC-TV's Sports Director Roone Arledge, sportscaster Jim McKay and Lamarque were together before the Preakness.

"Arledge said, 'Ronnie, if your horse wins the race, I might have you sing,'" Lamarque recalled. "I said, 'Mr. Arledge, with all due respect, if Star wins the race, I am singing.' And he and McKay laughed their butts off."

After the victory, Lamarque – a man who never met a microphone he didn't like — literally grabbed the mike out of McKay's hands and left an indelible impression on viewers when he belted out a Risen Star-styled version of "Way Down Yonder in New Orleans."

Lamarque's Risen Star partner was trainer Louie Roussel, a man of considerably fewer words. They were the odd couple, a sportswriter's dream: Lamarque a car salesman from Chalmette who owned horses named "Dese Days" and "Bridgin' Da Gap," and Roussel a devout Catholic known to be incredibly superstitious whose resume included lawyer, bank president and Fair Grounds owner.

"Louie and I, we're like brothers," Lamarque said.

Lamarque and Roussel made nationwide headlines and then they vanished from the national racing spotlight. They had a horse named Kandaly in 1994 that had some promise but turned out to be more a pretender than a contender. And that was it. The Louie and Ronnie show went on a seemingly permanent hiatus.

But on April 5 in the Illinois Derby at Hawthorne Race Course, they sent out the aptly named Recapturetheglory, with hopes of doing just that. Jockey E.T. Baird, son of Fair Grounds legend R.L. "Bobby" Baird, stormed his horse to the front and never looked back, winning by four lengths. Recapturetheglory had punched his ticket to Louisville on the first Saturday in May.

And now the horse is bedded down in Barn 41, Stall 17 at

Churchill Downs, the same barn and stall as Risen Star occupied in 1988.

"I was here with the best horse in America and lost in 1988," Roussel said. "We got a lot of hype and had such confidence, we didn't think he'd ever get beat.

"To come here with a longshot is a different thing. It's a tough task."

But although he could go off at odds of 20-1 or more at Saturday's Kentucky Derby, Recapturetheglory has a special name, Lamarque points out, almost as if the race was meant to be theirs. Roussel had been saving the name for the right horse.

"Louie told me, Ronnie, we want to recapture the glory that we lost with Star,'" Lamarque said. "We had the best horse in America, the world, and we never won the Derby."

But things are not exactly the same as in 1988.

For openers, both Roussel and Lamarque are 62. And Lamarque, the party guy, has found the Lord. The transformation came, he said, after his son Ronnie Jr. was born 11 years ago.

"I felt a change," Lamarque said. "That's when I went from being a Catholic to wanting to know more about the Holy Bible."

He went to Fellowship Bible Church to, as he put it, "learn the word of God and have a personal relationship with my Lord and Savior Jesus Christ." He says he has friends who now call him "a Jesus freak," but he's unfazed.

To boot, the party guy quit drinking alcohol more than a year ago.

"I drink Perrier. I still got thousand dollar bottles of wine that I give away. Somebody's gonna read this and want one," he joked.

Trying to reconcile horseracing and his religion gives him pause to reflect.

"Personally I look at it as a business and a game of chance, but would Jesus be in the horse business? I don't think so," Lamarque said. "So I have to live with that."

Lamarque's office on Williams Boulevard is a shrine to Risen Star and other horses he's raced. There's a story for every winner's circle picture, and few in horseracing have the memories of Triple

Crown winner's circles, so there are beaucoup tales to tell.

Comparing the two trips to Louisville,, Lamarque, said he expected a lot less pressure this time.

"You know how they say it's easier when you've been there the second time around, like the Super Bowl? I believe this is going to be a cinch."

During Derby week in 1988, he was out at the barn very early every morning, holding court with the media horde.

"I'm a tough guy, a strong guy. I can do that and then be ready for the Derby. But being up all night with the Whitneys and the parties – that won't happen this time."

Reporters expecting a song from the guy who was a member of the famed local cover band The Nobles may be disappointed.

"This is a real tough horse to write a song about," Lamarque said. "I believe the song days are over even though I'm a better singer now than I ever was. I just do 'To God Be the Glory' now – that's my song."

(Recapturetheglory, sent off at odds of 49-1, ran a remarkably good race, stayed with the winner in the stretch, finishing fifth behind winner Big Brown and the ill-fated filly Eight Belles.)

Not Your Normal Derby Flight

May 9, 1984

It was a typical Sunday morning after the Kentucky Derby. The weary, red-eyed crowd of handicappers and news media had flown from Louisville to the plane-changing capital of the world – Atlanta – and was boarding another Delta flight that would take them home to New Orleans.

A few seats in front of me, sportscaster Buddy Diliberto was taking a lot of ribbing for picking Althea in the race. In a field of 20, the favored Althea beat one horse. On the other side of the plane,

Wayne Krause of Mullet's News Stand was talking about the bet he made on the 78-1 longshot, Fight Over, who ran a big race, all things considered.

I buckled my seat belt and opened up the Louisville Courier-Journal. A small, elderly lady walked up and asked me if she had the right seat, which was next to the aisle seat. I assured her she did. She was very nervous as she sat down, had a hard time buckling her seat belt and finally said, "I don't fly very much." I smiled understandingly. A few moments later, the passenger who had the window seat arrived, and the lady was obviously uncomfortable as she got out and then back into her seat.

After much effort, we were all back where we belonged. The little lady took a deep breath, turned to me and said:

"I'm sorry. I'm a little shaky. I lost my husband yesterday."

"I'm terribly sorry," I told her.

Life deals some strange cards. Here in the midst of this planeload of tired Derby revelers was a woman who only 24 hours ago had been walking around the Epcot Center in Florida with her husband of 30 years after a sensational weeklong Caribbean cruise on a luxury liner. A day later, her mind was cluttered with thoughts about funeral arrangements, how she was going to find her relatives at the airport, and how she would carry on without her husband.

After the plane took off, our conversation resumed. We talked and we talked. This was not the way I had envisioned my flight home from the Derby, but then this was not the ride home from vacation that this lady had planned. In a world so short of compassion, what was an hour and 15 minutes of my time? When a fellow human being is in great need of talking to another person she has never seen before, it is time to listen. I did my best.

Sunny and Virginia Dugas were married for 30 years. They had no children, but had a good time with each other, especially since 1972 when Sunny retired. He had worked at the Monteleone Hotel as captain of the waiters and waitresses in the Carousel Bar. She had also worked, and retirement provided all the time in the world for what they loved to do most – travel.

They went everywhere – to Canada, to California, all over. They were Catholic, lived very near Schwegmann's on St. Claude, and her husband enjoyed his volunteer work in the Annunciation Church, also near their home. They liked their old neighborhood and found it convenient for their needs.

They were active in senior citizens' groups, and many of the trips they took were golden-ager tours. As best I can tell, Sunny and Virginia had the kind of relationship I would like to have at the same point in my life.

Several times during our talk, she said, "I'm sorry if I'm bothering you. I didn't mean to bend your ear. I don't talk much. I never did." I told her repeatedly I was enjoying talking to her.

"We had a wonderful cruise. We really did," she said. "The food was delicious. Oh, the food . . . We danced a lot. We loved to dance. One night the water was so rough it was hard to dance." The last part of the cruise, which had sailed out of Miami, included a day at Epcot. It was raining and they ran to a bench to get out of it. Sunny got a chill, and then he had a heart attack.

"He never had heart trouble. Never," she said. "He always exercised . . . " Her words trailed off, and she took a deep breath. I looked closely at her eyes, through the sunglasses she was wearing. She was trying to cry but she couldn't. She must have sensed my thoughts.

"It's funny," she said. "I can't cry. I get all choked up inside, but I can't. I've never been able to cry."

I told her I understood. We talked about when my dad died and how I felt, and I think that made her feel better. "I'll figure out some way to carry on," she said bravely.

"I know you will," I told her.

Sunny Dugas had something many of us do – a fear of flying. All of their many trips were taken on buses – even the ones to far-away places. Virginia had not been on a plane since 1959, when she and her father flew to pre-Castro Cuba.

"He simply wouldn't fly," she said. "It's funny . . . and now I'm flying him home."

CHAPTER 10
The Media

The Night They Roasted Buddy D

October 22, 2003

You expected some zingers from a colorful Cajun like former Saints quarterback Bobby Hebert. You knew you could count on America's favorite party animal QB, former Saints field general Billy Kilmer, for some comic relief.

And with master of ceremonies Jim Henderson cracking the jokes and the whip, you knew almost all of the roasters gathered last week for the "WWL 870-AM Roast of Buddy D" at the Keifer UNO Lakefront Arena would be on their worst behavior.

The wild card among the dozen or so speakers was former Saints Head Coach Jim Mora, a man not exactly known as a stand-up comic during his tenure here as the Saints all-time winningest coach. His adversarial relationship with Buddy D and other media types would hardly seem to make him a candidate for a wild and crazy night before a raucous audience.

In fact, he said, when he was asked to participate, he was stunned and then checked his calendar to make sure it wasn't April Fool's Day.

"We are gathered tonight to salute true greatness," Henderson began the evening with a wickedly impish smile on his face. "For it was Ralph Waldo Emerson who said, 'To be great is to be misunderstood.' We haven't understood Buddy Diliberto for 50 years."

When it was the gravel-voiced Kilmer's turn at the mike, Henderson said, "If you know Billy Kilmer's history, you know it's an absolute miracle that he was able to play quarterback in the NFL. How anyone could function with that much Absolut in him is a miracle . . . and probably explains why most of his passes looked like they did.

"Billy Kilmer left the Saints huddle in 1970. When Bobby Hebert first ducked his head in the Saints huddle in 1985, he said you could still smell the fumes."

"I always told people if you live in New Orleans, you gotta survive Bourbon Street and I did," said Kilmer, who described Buddy as "the second coming of Hap Glaudi," another local media legend who was known for his diction.

"I played with the early Saints and Buddy was always very kind to me. That's why me and Bobby Hebert, of all the quarterbacks who ever played here, that's why we're here 'cause none of those other guys would ever show up." But Kilmer did say that back in 1967, "I caught him and John Mecom hugging and holding hands."

Hebert, fit and trim and still with a deep Cajun accent, described himself as "kinda the Buddy D of Atlanta" because he does the Falcons post-game show. "Buddy always told it like it was and that's what I'm trying to do in Atlanta," he said. Hebert said he tries to be as passionate as Diliberto. "Buddy was always passionate even though maybe you couldn't understand him – but Atlanta can't understand me."

He said when new Saints players would come in, as the leader of the team they would ask him, "What's up with this Buddy Diliberto guy? Did he have a stroke or something?" Hebert said he would tell them, "No, he just has a hard time with Ws – he's kinda like the New Orleans male version of Barbara Walters."

Hebert closed by saying he couldn't find a bad word to say about Buddy.

When it was Mora's turn, it was as if he had been a regular on Comedy Central. "Bobby said he'd have a tough time finding something bad to say about Buddy. I find it very easy," Mora said. "The only thing that ticks me off is this: I get a few minutes up here to rip this guy and he ripped me for 11 years.

"Buddy was always on my offensive coordinator, Carl Smith. And I'm sure Buddy thought he could do a better job than Carl could. Can you imagine Buddy Diliberto calling a play in to Bobby

Hebert? And you know what the hell it would sound like by the time it got to our players? We would have been really screwed up. Of course, Buddy would have made Bobby sound like Richard Burton."

The other roasters included Richie Petibon, former Tulane and Chicago Bears star and former coach of the Washington Redskins; Dave Dixon, the father of the Louisiana Superdome; media figures such as Alec Gifford of WDSU-TV, Kenny Wilkerson of WWL, veteran sportscaster Vince Marinello, Times-Picayune sports columnist Pete Finney, and on video in absentia, Archie Manning. Near the end, Abdul D. Tentmakur gave an encore performance of "Buddy Be Good."

Wilkerson gave the crowd a lesson on Dilibonics. "You don't have to go back through the years, you only have to listen for a night or two, that's all the material you need," he said. "Just the other day at the game, he paused 10 seconds for station idefecation."

Then, in order, Wilkerson mentioned these Buddyesque names: Won Saboda, Tyle Kurley and Chris Canole, who used to play for the Saints; Saints general manager Misty Loomis; Stoot in the Morning; the band Len-yard Skin-yard; and "one of our counterparts in crime, Hokie Gajan, or as Buddy would say sometimes, Cokie Gajan or Hokie Saigon. The best was when he said, 'Let's go back down to Thibodaux live with Kenny Wilker and Honkie Gajan.' "

Gifford and Buddy D worked together at Channel 8 WVUE from 1967 through 1980. "Historians at Channel 8," said Henderson, "refer to that time as the Golden Era of New Orleans television . . . the Golden Era for Channel 4, Channel 6 and Channel 26."

Gifford said: "Buddy Diliberto is the only person I know in the television business who is out of lip sync when he's live."

In between speakers, there were video bites to surprise Buddy, who was greatly amused by them. One of those came from Saints wide receiver Donte Stallworth: "Hey, Buddy, this is Donte Stallworth. That's Stallworth, not Stallpepper."

Petibon and Buddy's dads both worked at The Times-Picayune. Richie, a lifelong pal, said Buddy is known for two things – getting fired every time the Super Bowl is in town and No. 2, getting barred for life plus ten years on the Saints charter flight.

Both avid horseplayers, he said they were at a racing book in Lake Tahoe, betting horses all day, starting on the East Coast in New York and winding up in the west at Santa Anita. When it was getting near dinnertime, the manager came over and asked Buddy if he liked abalone. "Buddy was busy studying the Racing Form," said Petibon, "and he looked up and says, 'Is he at Santa Anita? Who's riding?' "

Archie Manning sent his video apologies for his absence and you knew Henderson was going to cover for his missing sidekick. Manning, he said, "was going to be here tonight until he found out that he couldn't get a free sport coat from Joe Gemelli's for being here after all. So he decided to do what he usually does on Thursday nights: Stay home, get all liquored up and count Peyton's money.

"Actually, Archie couldn't be here tonight because he's in Oxford, Mississippi . . . counting the money Eli's going to make."

Finney's tale dated back to 1961 when he, Buddy and then WWL sports director Lou Boda were driving to New York to see the Mickey Mantle-Roger Maris home run race, with Maris hitting 61 to top Babe Ruth's record of 60.

With Buddy at the wheel, they got pulled over for speeding in a small town in Virginia and the cop led them to a service station, where they were instructed to go into the back room, which turned out to be the "courthouse."

Said Finney: "The guy who was pumping gas shows up in black robes. He's the judge. Buddy says, 'I think we're in trouble.'" He asks Buddy what his name is and he says, Bernard S. Diliberto. The judge says this is Virginia and we don't take initials. What does the S stand for? Buddy still refuses to say.

Finally he realizes he has to and blurts out, "Saverio." Whereupon Boda starts laughing out loud and the judge fines Boda $25. Buddy had to pay a $50 fine. Boda said it was worth every penny to find out what Buddy's middle name was.

Then Finney recalled the time in 1980, the year the Saints were 1-15, Diliberto invites Finney onto his TV show and tells him he's got a big surprise. He was sitting on a bag and in the middle of the show puts on the bag and tells Pete he's going to wear it until the

Saints won a game. "The second half of the show he had the bag on his head. Can you imagine trying to understand Diliberto with a bag on his head?"

Mora trashed Buddy for his evaluation of Mike Ditka's coaching talents and his predictions of what a great coach he was going to be. In his rebuttal, Buddy said of Mora, "I wish he would have stayed a little longer because then my tombstone wouldn't say, 'He recommended Ditka.' "

After the roast ended, Diliberto said Mora was "as funny as I've ever seen him. You know, at the time, under the pressure cooker that sports is today, you understand why some things are said. It's an adversarial position. But once the players and coaches get out of the sport and there's not as much friction going on, they're good guys, just regular guys.

"Bottom line, I was well pleased. I knew that the guys who are in the same business, my colleagues, would come through. But to get Kilmer and Hebert and Mora to come in made me feel good."

At one point, Mora put his hand on Buddy's shoulder and told him he'd lost a lot of weight and looked good. "That's what happens when you cover the Saints for 37 years," he replied.

The roast ended with a typically droll comment from the master of ceremonies: "A copy of Buddy's remarks translated into English is available."

(The beloved Buddy Diliberto died in January of 2005. In April that year, his show was taken over by Bobby Hebert.)

"Holy Cow! Man Alive! Oh Brother! Hold the Phone!"

July 23, 2000

When young Bruce Miller first heard Harry Caray broadcasting St. Louis Cardinals games on KMOX, he remembers saying to himself, "Listen to this guy – he's sounds like a damn fan – he'll say anything!"

Tulane football fans who listened to "Bronco" Bruce Miller do the Green Wave's play-by-play broadcast for years wouldn't at all be surprised to hear Miller say that "Harry was one of my biggest influences."

Miller even used Caray's legendary "Holy cow!" pronouncement from time to time but he had his own Miller-esque repertoire which amused, entertained and occasionally baffled the Wave faithful listening to him and his sidekick Wayne Mack describing the action over the airwaves.

"Man alive!" was one of Miller's chief exclamations, but "Oh brother!" was easily his most frequently used expression — and it served him well for a variety of situations. "Looney flushed out of the pocket, he's under severe pressure, now he's going to pass, long and deep, a man is open! Oh brother!" he would say, and no one, of course, save those who had a crystal ball, knew whether the pass was complete, complete but fumbled, incomplete or intercepted.

"Oh brother!" would then give way to "Hold the phone!" – which Wave fans knew was Miller's way to break bad news. "Hold the phone!" through the years became synonymous with fumbles lost, touchdown passes called back, interceptions, penalty flags, dropped balls and assorted other disasters.

Giants broadcaster Russ Hodges will forever be remembered for his legendary call of New York Giant Bobby Thompson's home run in the bottom of the ninth to beat the Brooklyn Dodgers at the Polo Grounds in the final game of a playoff series in 1951: "The Giants win the pennant! The Giants win the pennant!"

ABC's Al Michaels will never be forgotten for his call of the final moments of the overachieving and outmanned U.S. Hockey team's upset of Russia in the 1980 Olympics: "Do you believe in miracles? Yes!"

The defining moment of Miller's career came on Dec. 1, 1973, at old Tulane Stadium on Willow Street. With 86,000 fans in attendance, a Tulane team that had not beaten LSU for 24 years held an insurmountable 14-0 lead over the Tigers with a minute and 37 seconds left and the clock winding down. Over the crowd's deafening roar, Mack shouted into the mike: "The Greenies have the football and the football game!"

Then it was Miller's turn.

"The long, long dry spell, the long hot summers, the long hot winters are over, as the Greenies have broken it . . . There never was a New Year's Eve like this, Wayne! Never! 'Holy cow!' as Harry Caray says! Oh man alive!"

He said, "long hot winters" – and nobody even blinked.

Bronco Bruce Miller quietly retired from WWL last week after 20 years with that station and 43 years broadcasting both on radio and TV in New Orleans.

"That game was so unbelievable," he recalled this week. "All of us felt something big was going to happen.

"The energy that night, the atmosphere was charged with electricity. Just walking in up the ramps you could feel it. There was no place for me ever like Tulane Stadium. I miss that old place even to this day. They tore the heart out of the university when they tore that place down."

As a boy growing up in Geneva, Ill., Miller wanted to be a baseball player for the Chicago White Sox – "another Nellie Fox, but I wasn't good enough." A career guidance counselor told him, "Bruce, you've got a good voice – why don't you try radio?"

"As a kid I used to broadcast make-believe games in my bedroom at night. The Sox always beat the Yankees in the bottom of the ninth. So I was preparing for a career without even knowing about it."

After a stint in the military with Armed Forces radio in Germany, he arrived in New Orleans in December of 1957. An on-air stint at the old WDSU radio station led to weekend sports reporting on WDSU-TV and not long after that, he became the radio voice of the Wave, first with Eddie Price, then Moon Mullins and finally, the man he wanted, Wayne Mack.

"What we did most was entertain," said Miller.

No doubt about it. From the late '50s through 1976, Miller and Mack had moments that every comedy team from Martin and

Lewis to Cheech and Chong would be proud of. Undoubtedly, Miller's most famous "Oh brother!" took place during the Duke game in Durham in 1973. In the final minute with the score tied, 17-17, Tulane quarterback Steve Foley threw a touchdown pass to his brother, Mike Foley, as the game ended. Miller shouted, "Oh brother! Brother-to-brother!"

When things got slow, as they did far too often, Miller and Mack would digress. During one Tulane-Georgia Bulldogs game, there was a discussion about why bulldogs' tails are short and whether they can wag. At a blowout at Rutgers, when it started snowing, there were musings on the size and shape of snowflakes and how no two are alike. And at West Virginia, they were talking about the Mountaineer campus being located on the banks of the beautiful Monongahela River, and a geography lesson broke out.

Listeners soon learned that the Monongahela is one of the few rivers in the world that flows from south to north, and while the kickoff was underway, they found out that the Nile in Egypt also flows from south to north.

But what you lived for were the moments when they turned from announcers to fans. When a Tulane pass fell incomplete against Miami and they thought there had been obvious pass inter-ference, Miller said, "I think these officials came equipped from the dog tracks tonight with blinkers." Mack concurred, saying the Miami defensive back had the Wave receiver "around the waist like he was measuring him up for a suit."

Miller also occasionally used ballet terms, such as pirouette and adagio, to describe fancy footwork moves. And his explanations sometimes needed a further review: "Allright, it's Foley at quarter-back – quickie pass to Frank Anderson – aw – fumbles the ball – he kicks it and it – who's got it? Boston College – big pileup on the football – and the ball goes out of bounds. What happened was Frank Anderson on a look-in – a quickie pass – he dropped the ball off the turf and then kicked it with his foot, and the ball went soar-ing out of bounds after several players touched it – now let's see what the decision will be as to who has it, and I think it's going to be ruled – simply – what?"

Miller got the nickname "Bronco Bruce" from a horse by that name that was running on a media day gathering at the Fair Grounds. It stuck mainly because Mack persisted in calling him that and Miller didn't seem to mind.

Unabashedly and emotionally tied to Tulane during his broadcast years, when a Jim Pittman-coached team lost to Florida, 18-17, on a last-second two-point conversion pass from John Reaves to Carlos Alvarez, "I cried. I broke down in tears," he said. "Tulane outplayed them so badly. It was so unfair."

After Tulane decided to go in a new, but misguided direction in the mid-'70s, and severed its ties with Miller and Mack, it was Hap Glaudi who got WWL radio to hire Miller, and it was there what he calls "the most enjoyable thing I did in my whole career" took place. After Wayne Mack's 6-8 p.m. talk show, Miller did an 8-midnight free flow show, which was some music, some talk.

"It was probably my most satisfying moment, and it was not in sports."

Another favorite Tulane moment came at Lubbock, Texas, in 1960. "Two first team All-Americans, Tommy Mason and E.J. 'The Beast' Holub, their linebacker, they came together head-to-head all afternoon," he said. "It was a hard-fought game, they both went on to be first round draft choices and all-pros. Tech won but after the game Holub came out to the Tulane bus and congratulated Tommy. It was a colossal game."

Through the years, one of Miller's favorites away from Tulane football was Saints tight end Hoby Brenner, "as modest and unassuming guy as there was, who had no ego at all and would sit and talk to you forever." And then there was Jim Finks. "We were both from Illinois and we hit it off like brothers. I loved the man. I had such respect for him. He made every reporter feel like they were special."

Jim Mora, on the other hand, was "one of the most difficult people to be around. There was no way you could win. You couldn't ask him anything."

When Miller first got started in broadcasting, he said, "I was going to be the best there ever was, just like 'The Natural.' I fell far short of that but that's okay – that's the way you're supposed to start out. Right now I'm so clearly aware of the many wonderful things that have happened to me, and all through the grace of God. I believe that with all my heart."

Bruce Miller is 69. He considers himself lucky because he got to work with Wayne Mack, Hap Glaudi and Buddy Diliberto.

"Hap, even at the end, was still so enthusiastic and into it. Buddy's like that too. I'm not. I don't have it like I once did. But I know this – I will miss being behind the mike. We had a lot of fun."

Oh brother! Did they ever! Man alive!

The Ol' Redhead and His Kiddies

April 29, 1977

Roll back the clock to the late '40s. You are sitting in front of your Emerson radio, sipping a Regal beer, waiting for a familiar voice.

There is crowd noise, only a trace of a scratchy recording, the chatter of beer and peanut vendors. Then comes the crack of a bat and the strains of "Take Me Out to the Ball Game." Then the resonant, rapid-fire voice:

"Good evening, baseball fans. It's a beautiful night in Nashville, perfect for baseball. The Pels have just finished infield practice, and the grounds crew at Sulphur Dell is going over the baseball paths right now. We'll have live action in a few minutes."

Unmistakably, it is Ted Andrews, the master of diamond drama. Can it be more than three decades since we first heard the Ol' Redhead? How long since Evolution and his "I-gotta-gotta-gotta peeeee-nuts?" Remember the Knothole Gang and 10-cent programs advertising chicken dinners at Delicate Jerry's, Slacks from Nowak's, Dixie "45" beer, and the Rockery Inn?

Yes, it can. Ted Andrews is now 72. And the last time we heard him end a baseball game with his trademark – "Good night to all of you and a special good night to you kiddies" – was 1959, when the Pels bid a sad adieu to New Orleans at City Park, a football stadium, before 300 fans.

Tomorrow night from the Louisiana Superdome, Andrews, after spending spring training in St. Petersburg with the Pelicans and their parent club, the St. Louis Cardinals, once again will be in the pressbox.

It is only justice that Andrews is again part of the Pelicans organization, and as he sits inside the plush Superdome, fond memories will surely pass in review: Engel Stadium, where the Chattanooga Lookouts held court; Ponce de Leon, where Atlanta's Crackers dwelt; and the rest of the Southern Association: the Birmingham Barons, Memphis Chicks, Mobile Bears, Nashville Vols and Little Rock Travelers.

"Last night, the Pels moved closer to first place by whipping the Vols in their own backyard, 9-8," the Emerson crackles. "And if Al Flair keeps swinging the bat the way he has been, and manager Fred Walters keeps playing, then you can look for the Pels to take another one tonight.

"They call Walters 'The Whale' because of his size, you know, but last night he pegged out four runners trying to steal second base, and that's not bad. I believe the Vols will be hanging closer to first tonight. Anyway, we'll be back with the action right after I tell you about Coca-Cola, our sponsor."

Andrews is sitting behind a WJBW mike, one of five stations he will broadcast Pels games for, the others being WTPS, WDSU, WNOE and WWEZ. But he is not at Sulphur Dell in Nashville – he is in the Audubon Building on Canal Street. It is a hot, humid night in the Crescent City, unlike the perfect night for baseball in Nashville Andrews has his listeners thinking about.

The game hasn't begun yet, and Andrews is soaking wet from perspiration. He takes off his shirt and will broadcast the game in his undershirt. There is a big fan in the small studio, but it is far enough away from the Redhead that the mike doesn't pick up the hum of the motor. At the Redhead's elbow is a Western Union operator. Up at Sulphur Dell, there is another.

The game is now under way. Over ticker tape in code, the operator taps out: "S1C, B1O," and Andrews goes into his chatter:

"Mel Rue at the plate. Well, the little banjo hitter's been getting good wood on the ball lately and we'll see what he does tonight. The pitcher toes the rubber, winds, and here's the pitch. Strike one called!"

It was never difficult for Andrews to re-create, or fake, a broadcast. "S1C" was strike one called. "B1O' was ball one outside, and so on. In front of him was a diagram of the stadium, and he had done his homework: he knew pitchers' quirks, batters' traits – whether the pitcher brushed back batters, picked up dirt, tugged at his cap, whether the batter dug in or bailed out.

He used no gimmicks, no blocks of wood slamming together to sound like a double, no tricks. An engineer had a crowd noise record, and through a window Andrews would use finger cues to raise the sound level for a home run, lower it for a walk.

He knew Chattanooga pitcher Bobo Newsome couldn't pitch if there were pieces of paper around the mound. So if the wire was slow coming in, he would go into a monologue about Newsome's superstitions and how Pel outfielder Paul Smith carried paper around in his back pocket to drop near the mound and aggravate Newsome.

"The minute I hit that mike I was an actor. But I was also a reporter. I never tried to fool anybody, but I had done my homework, and I could fill in the rain delays," Andrews said.

He got weather reports before the game and knew when the wind was blowing in or out, whether the basepaths had been heavily watered if the home team was hosting a base-stealing team, whether the grass had been cut or allowed to grow.

The rest was Ted's imagination, 100 percent. "I tried to keep within 30 seconds of the ball or strike, or hit. Plenty places had tickers, and I didn't want to still be broadcasting when the game was over."

When Red Barrett was throwing strikes, Ted knew he was throwing "a heavy ball." He couldn't see him but he knew the spitball was his best pitch. When Walker Cress was pitching on a really hot

169

night, he knew he was having trouble with his wrists. Even though Cress was born in Baton Rouge, he couldn't handle hot weather and had to soak his wrists in ice water before games.

It's been told too many times, but the best Ted Andrews story is his re-creation of the dialogue between manager Rip Sewell and outfielder Filipe Montemayor. Montemayor had charged a line drive that went over his head in the first game of a twi-night doubleheader, and when Sewell asked for a reason, Filipe said, "The sun got me."

When it happened again that night, Sewell asked, "Was it the moon?"

Tomorrow night, it'll be the Omaha Royals instead of the Nashville Vols. And in weeks to come, it'll be the Oaks, Bears, Triplets, 89ers, Indians and Aeros instead of the Barons, Chicks, Crackers and the rest.

It'll be the Dome instead of Pel Stadium at Carrollton and Tulane. And you'll have to drive to Matt Lehrmann's Home Plate Inn instead of walking across Tulane Avenue from the ballpark.

But it'll still be Pel baseball to me, and even if he doesn't say it, I'll always remember the Ol' Redhead saying, "And a special good night to you kiddies."

I was one of 'em.

The Oldie King & the Traffic Dude

December 10, 2005

For sheer radio entertainment that almost made you drive off the road with tears of laughter, they were as good as it gets — afternoon going-home host Oldie King Bob Walker and his "traffic dude in a traffic mood," the legendary Sgt. T-Ben Boudreaux.

From 1989-1992, Walker and T-Ben kicked butt on Oldies 106.7 – among the first FM stations in New Orleans to play oldies — with King Bob the setup man and Boudreaux throwing the knockout punches.

Boudreaux, wearing torn blue jeans with a piece of rope for a belt, mirrored sunglasses, a coonskin cap and a shirt emblazoned with sergeant's stripes, became a household name and Walker captured the New Orleans mentality as no station had since WTIX-AM ruled the New Orleans radio airwaves in the '60s.

The hyperactive Boudreaux saw himself as the supreme and exalted commander of traffic flow, aided by a runaway ego that made him truly believe he was exactly that – a "modern day traffic hero," by his own admission.

"Think of the Causeway Bridge as a symphony! Think of me as the conductor!" he would say. "Listen to me – I'll set you free!"

Typical of radio, which changes formats and ownership more than Peyton Manning changes plays, the station was sold, the budget was slashed and T-Ben and his coonskin cap were out the door.

Walker eventually resurfaced at WTIX-FM-94.3, the call letters of the AM station where he had spent most of his time behind a mike since 1965. In the spring of 2002, after dedicating his life to New Orleans music and oldies, he packed it in, totally disgusted and disillusioned with bottom-line corporate radio that neutered playlists and couldn't care less about the betterment of music.

But that was then and this is now. And never say never.

"I was determined that I was done," Walker said. "Believe me."

But his house in Mississippi blew away so he didn't have anyplace to watch sunsets. People stopped him on the street and said they wished he'd come back. "I saw people so down about the hurricane, people that needed to laugh," he said. "So I thought, if I can bring 'em a little happiness, why not?"

He and Boudreaux approached station manager Michael Costello about the possibility of resurrecting some history and . . .

Last week, Walker went back on the air on WTIX-FM from 3 p.m. to 7 p.m. and T-Ben is expected to join him on Monday. They had talked through the years about re-creating the magic. "It's the only scenario that would bring us back," Walker said. And if this city ever needed an uplift, well, here it comes.

"We have a great vehicle for our gig because it's a great New

Orleans station," Boudreaux said. "Michael has the biggest music library there is. It's a great local treasure."

When you hear Walker asking T-Ben what's playing at the adult movie house near the Chef overpass over I-10, and Boudreaux responds, "King Bob, it's Aaron Broussard in 'Hair Today, Gone Tomorrow!'" you'll know the past is now the present.

And when the sounds of "wham-bam traffic jam" and "creep-and-crawl, y'all" fill the airways, you'll know, as Walker says, "that the sound and the spirit of old New Orleans are alive today. We just want to bring back some fun in the afternoon – and we're both excited about it."

Walker sees himself as Ed McMahon and Sgt. T-Ben as Johnny Carson. "I'm just the grease that keeps it going. T-Ben is Robin Williams on speed. He's always been ahead of his time, or any time."

"If we are going to rebuild the city, I must be the first brick," Boudreaux said, "and King Bob will be the mortar. He's come out of retirement more times than Hulk Hogan."

Between Jefferson Parish President Broussard, Saints owner Tom Benson, Mayor Ray Nagin, Gov. Kathleen Blanco and a cast of thousands, Boudreaux said thinking about what will be playing at the adult movie theater near the high rise "literally keeps me awake at night. I keep a pad by my bed. That adult movie thing taught me how to write jokes."

He apparently learned his lessons well – he has been writing jokes for Jay Leno and other radio stations for years.

"With these clowns, I've got enough material for adult movie signs through 2008," he said. "Now comes the fun."

"The traffic report is just an excuse for him being there," said Walker. "Nobody ever paid attention to his traffic reports – no more than they watched Morgus for scientific reality."

Boudreaux would watch the traffic monitors but he enjoyed winging it a lot more. "Yahoo! OK, King Bob, eastbound on the Huey, I'm beginning to see some heavy traffic and here's some evidence: At the local convenience stores in Avondale, they're out of the tall Old Milwaukees!"

"Oh no, West Bank! The bridge that set you free has enslaved you again. It's wham-bam traffic jam!"

Boudreaux said that when he would do remotes, people would come up to him and tell him that he gave the best and most accurate traffic information – and Boudreaux would think to himself, "My God, what an idiot."

The new show will be "duplicated exactly from the old show. It's going to be the way we did it before, the way we know works," Walker said. "It'll be like Morgus going back with Eric and Chopsley. We talked about it for years – now the time is right."

(Walker has since retired again. Sgt. T-Ben Boudreaux, aka Ben Walsh, is still writing jokes for Jay Leno and does the "news" for WTIX-FM.)

Chase & Dufour: Historians for the Ages

April 20, 1986

As long as I live, I'll never forget the day I went to lunch at Christian's restaurant with Iberville and Bienville.

Most folks called them Chase and Dufour, but by the time I finished polishing off crawfish etouffee and a bottle of wine, I was convinced I had indeed dined with the founding fathers of New Orleans. No one else could possibly have known as much about the early history of this settlement.

As a team, John Churchill Chase and Charles L. "Pie" Dufour were without parallel as local historians emeritus. Chase, cartoonist extraordinaire for decades – first for newspapers, later for television – wrote the definitive book on New Orleans street names ("Frenchmen, Desire, Good Children") and for years taught a history course with Dufour at Tulane University. Pie referred to it as "New Orleans on the half shell."

Dufour, whose regular column, "A la Mode," was a mainstay of the afternoon newspapers, is an author of numerous books on the Civil War as well as "Ten Flags in the Wind: The Story of Louisiana," and a Carnival buff of the highest order. When Chase and Dufour were both hired by The States in the late 1940s, it was a coup.

Former States-Item Editor Walter G. Cowan said, "In bowling, it was a 300 game."

Ever since I dined with these gentlemen about a decade ago – and listened to them argue with each other over the fine points of New Orleans history and culture – I have never been able to think of one without the other.

Until this week when John Chase died.

Chase, a graduate of Isidore Newman School and the Chicago Academy of Fine Arts, left so many indelible marks on this city that Orleanians will recall him for a variety of reasons: his signature on the animated television cartoons that appeared on WDSU-TV from 1964 to 1974; his chief cartoon character, the representative of the people, the little man dressed in an 1890s long-coat, top hat, bushy moustache and glasses; and the dry wit that pervades his book on street names.

I'll remember him for all of those things, but one of his endeavors still stands out, possibly because he did it during the impressionable years of my youth: all those great covers of Tulane football programs. No matter how bad things were going on the field – and they usually were – Chase's cartoons depicted a surreptitious Greenie football player with a wicked smile somehow outwitting his bigger, stronger opponent by setting a trap or bamboozling him.

If nothing else, it provided a chuckle and eternal hope to the courageous few who attended games on Willow Street.

Chase's humor showed up not only in his illustrations and drawings but also in his observations of his own work. In the preface to his book, he thanked many people, including his wife, "who," he wrote, "says she does so believe that I was at the library all the times I said I was at the Sazerac Bar. I also wish to thank the bartenders of the Sazerac Bar."

When I asked him to tell me about the awards he had received for his cartoons, he deadpanned. "I won awards for everything but drawing cartoons. I was second in the Pulitzer Prize one year, but that's like coming out second in a duel. I even won the state fencing championship one year. They couldn't figure me out – nobody ever saw a left-handed fencer."

As Chase's book on streets drew acclaim, his luncheon lecture calendar filled up. He talked about the origin of street names so much, he felt he was an original pothole. "I do not think," he told me, "that anyone has ever spoken from the platform more about the same subject without either being elected or defeated in public office."

Chase's and Dufour's paths crossed early in life. As schoolboys, Chase lived on Robert Street and had to walk past Dufour's house on Valmont to get to Newman, while Pie was readying himself for the trek to Jesuit. Their careers paralleled each other, although Pie was a couple of years his senior. They were close friends, and enjoyed untold moments of point-counterpoint debating their love, the history of New Orleans.

But as similar as their interests and pursuits were, their daily lifestyles were on opposite ends of the spectrum. They discussed this from time to time, and once, I was with them.

"I'm an early riser," Chase said. "I got up at a quarter to 3 today. It's a creative time, no telephones. I'm through at 10."

"Chase," replied Pie, "you're the darndest Dawn Patrol man I ever saw. I like it the other way around. I stay up until 1 or 2 in the morning reading. I don't see how you do it."

"That," said Chase, "is what makes horse races."

A Prince Among Thieves

December 16, 2008

For more than 35 years he was this newspaper's chief blood-hound, sleuthing around the Crescent City, checking in on murder

175

scenes, working the phone with detectives, driving around in a car that never stopped at car washes, his constant companions a back seat full of old notepads, newspapers, bank statements and a hamper full of dirty clothes.

Neither "rumpled" or "scruffy" adequately describes the mismatched wardrobe of Walt Philbin, a sartorial throwback to the newspapering days of Damon Runyon. His one concession to fashion was a seasonal fedora – felt in the winter, straw in the summer, missing only a card stuck in the headband reading, "Press."

Walter J. Philbin Jr., my colleague who made TV's wrinkled-trenchcoat-wearing Lt. Columbo look like a GQ model, has retired from The Times-Picayune, leaving a huge void. A living legend with a degree from the old school of rough-and-tumble journalism, he had an amazing knack for observing details, a rapport few have with sources, and most importantly, the uncanny ability to get information that others could not.

Interviewing is an art form, a gift some reporters have and others do not. A good interviewer is like a surgeon, delicately extracting bits and pieces after gaining someone's confidence, getting them to relax, putting them at ease, even in the toughest, most traumatic situations. In the media world the disarming Philbin was not just a surgeon, he was a top-flight neurosurgeon, his halting, soft-spoken commiserative approach almost always getting the information he wanted – and more.

Like Peter Falk's legendary Columbo character, he was non-threatening, seemingly befriending the people he was questioning. And like the detective, you can almost hear him saying, "Just one more thing . . . "

For years he hung out at the Miracle Mile on South White Street near Tulane and Broad, waiting for verdicts to come in, cultivating the trust of cops and prosecutors who frequented that bar. His competitiveness with rival media found him developing unconventional ways of getting stories. He got an assistant district attorney to give him a hand signal – two fingers to his temple — coming out of the grand jury room where a double murder indictment had been handed down in a famed honeymoon murder case. He beat his competition to the story, befuddling rival journalists.

"Those are the moments you live for — more than awards — when everything's hitting on all cylinders," Philbin said. "You know you're in the zone."

His boundless enthusiasm for a particular case, no matter how gruesome, was contagious in the newsroom. He talked incessantly. In the old days before emails and cell phones, he often cradled two telephones – one up for listening, one down for talking – always a bit on the loud side in the newsroom.

New hires were taken aback by the sight of a colleague wearing a well-worn blazer or tattered trench coat with its pockets stretched to the limit by notebooks, pens, an alarm clock and various sundries he carried around with him at all times – the unpressed, unshaved look, often having slept in a car during a stakeout — the alarm clock to awaken him if he fell asleep.

But they soon met a very sensitive, caring person, a Vietnam veteran who was a forward observer and saw action, a pretty fair boxer in his day, a tap dancer wannabe, a rare bird who ironically had a penchant for bird watching, a Tulane sports fan and a hard worker with a fire in his belly who put in long hours and was willing to help young reporters.

Philbin came into the local news scene – after a stint at the Jackson Clarion-Ledger — as a cub reporter for the old States-Item afternoon paper in January of 1973, hired by editor Walter Cowan. At that time there were some outstanding hard-nosed newsmen working for the S-I, guys like Tom Gregory, Jack Wardlaw and Cowan himself.

Assistant city editor Billy Rainey, the king of the re-write men, took Philbin under his wing and became the biggest influence on Philbin's career. Rainey would listen to Philbin calling in incredible details and pertinent quotes on everything from crime scenes to explosions, drownings, fires, bank robberies, kidnappings, whatever — and then Rainey would get to typing, sorting out everything and getting it into print for the final street edition while Philbin kept calling back with more information.

On one infamous occasion, Philbin came back into the newsroom very animated after covering some story and Rainey asked him, "Whatcha got, Walt?" Philbin pulled out a notebook, looked down at his illegible chicken scratch, began to stammer and stutter and was running all the facts together in his inimitable stream of consciousness free-flow, out-of-order sequence. His mouth had betrayed him.

So Rainey, ever resourceful, took a drag on his cigarette and shouted at him: "Philbin, go back to your desk and pick up the phone!"

"No," Walt continued, "but you know, and then, but after, but before, I mean, this is what happened, and then they . . . "

"Philbin, dammit. Get back to your desk and pick up the (bleeping) phone!" Rainey shouted.

Philbin dutifully headed back to his desk, mumbling and muttering the whole way. When he got to his desk, he picked up the phone.

Rainey shouted across the newsroom, "Now call me!"

Which is what Philbin did. Back then, we were all much more comfortable dictating from the field, and he was much better on the phone. The words flowed, he had his facts, the best re-write guy put it into a story, and the two miraculously met another tough deadline amidst a loud, raucous and sometimes tense newsroom — where people smoked cigars and cigarettes, cussed and yelled, and laughed and drank together after work . . . and sometimes during.

"He taught me how to be a newspaperman," said Philbin, adding that Rainey called him "a knucklehead" frequently. "He was the biggest influence on my career. He used to say, 'Don't call me a journalist – I'm a newspaperman and what I do is newspapering.' But we clicked, we really clicked."

At that time, there were two old-time police and crime reporters that some called "The Gold Dust Twins," police reporter Jack Dempsey and his sidekick Bert Hyde, both with loud stentorian voices. Those who knew Dempsey, a cigar-chomping, hat-wearing Irishman from the Channel who operated out of police headquarters, see some Dempsey in Philbin – which is not surprising, since Philbin worked many stories with Dempsey.

"Dempsey taught me a lot about unconventional ways to get stories," he said, "like sitting in a judge's office, just shooting the breeze and picking up on things like cases that might be coming up."

In the 1970s there was a sensational case where a priest, his housekeeper and a nun were brutally murdered in an Edgard rectory and a caretaker was pistol-whipped at the altar. "Philbin was all over it," said colleague John Pope, who was also there. "He relayed someone's observation that the moon came out blood-red that night. And when a bunch of newsies showed up at someone's house for an interview, Walt hung back.

"When the throng left after getting next to nothing, Walt sidled up to the front door and, in his best halting Jimmy Stewart-style, he commiserated, and, after a long preamble, asked what it was like to see all that blood. He got answers. That was his way."

Then there were the moments that solidified Philbin's eccentric reputation. Political writer Frank Donze accompanied Philbin on what was one of his first dates with a reporter named Molly Moore. "We went out to eat and drove from the paper in one car," said Donze. "While we were eating, his beeper goes off, he runs to the pay phone and when he returns, he asked Molly and me to pack up our food in a to-go container because we had to rush over to Central Lockup to bail out one of his female cousins who had gotten into a bar fight.

"Molly always used to talk about that night as one of the most interesting dates she ever had as the two of us watched him interact with all the people inside and outside the jail who knew him so well."

"I remember how Walt often tried to win over the 'new girl' in the newsroom by taking her on a tour of New Orleans' bloodiest crime scenes," said colleague Lynne Jensen. "I've heard tell that at some spots he would escort her from the car to search for remaining blood stains.

"And some say romance is dead."

Then there was the time another assistant city editor, Gene Mearns, sent Boomer (Philbin's nickname) out around 6 a.m. to cover the report of a fire in an Uptown double. Boomer came back an hour later and said there was nothing to it.

"Guy fell asleep smoking," Philbin said, "lots of smoke, no flames, no injury, nothing."

Mearns insisted on some copy. So Philbin sat down and wrote: "Fire claimed an Uptown couch this morning."

The tables were turned one year in an episode where Philbin himself was the victim, and the cops came to his house after he was burglarized.

They looked at each other and one commented, "Gee, Walt, they really ransacked the place." To which Walt replied, "Oh no, they didn't touch anything. They just took my TV."

Not that long ago, Philbin walked into the newsroom with a dead rattlesnake in a plastic bag. It had been evidence in a case in which a man was killed while transporting the snake on the back of a motorcycle, got distracted by the snake and struck a curb. Philbin thought it ought to be given a proper burial.

Nobody even blinked – that was Walt.

Assistant to the Editor Lynn Cunningham worked with him at the States-Item. Pregnant, she was due on Mardi Gras in 1989.

"Walter was particularly concerned about how I would get to Touro Infirmary to deliver my baby," she said. "His concern grew into something short of panic as I rolled in every day. He had several routes worked out for me to get to the hospital based on parade routes and times.

"What truly panicked him, though, was the thought that I would go into labor in the newsroom. He fretted about this."

Everything worked out, and Philbin was her first visitor outside the family, bringing a Mother's roast beef po-boy to her husband.

"The older I get the firmer I believe that the measure of a person is taken in what he does, but doesn't have to do," she said. "What I will remember most is the gentleman that Philbin was and is."

Of all the stories I worked with Walt – and there were many – one stands out because it was so memorable and so much fun. On September 15, 1978, we covered the Muhammad Ali-Leon Spinks heavyweight championship bout at the Superdome. Assigned to do the crowd story, Walt and I were on opposite sides of the ring, communicating by walkie-talkie.

It was a circus atmosphere as Ali sought to regain his crown, which he did. There was a hookers' convention in town and they were very visible at the fight. Right after the third bout on the card, a woman in a slinky red dress entered the ring, unfurled her raven hair . . . and stripped. It turned out to be porno star Edy Williams, eventually covered up and escorted off.

"I don't know why they stopped it," was the quote Philbin got from a boxing fan.

Philbin knows he will go through some newsman's withdrawal.

"Where did all the years go? Unbelievable. How many young reporters have I gone to murder scenes with? I'm going to miss it, emotionally and physically, but I'm leaving things in good hands. Brendan McCarthy, Laura Maggi, Leslie Williams, they know what they're doing.

"It's time. I still want to write, maybe for myself, even if it's just memories of precious years."

There's going to be a blowout for Walt where stories will abound. One that will be told and re-told for years is this: McCarthy is taking Walt to Meyer the Hatter where his newsroom colleagues are purchasing him a new fedora. The old one will be enshrined in the newsroom, in a glass case – right over the police radios.

CHAPTER 11
Everyday Life

Empty Nest Trial Run

August 25, 1995

For the past week or so, my wife and I have gotten a preview of what life is going to be for us in about a year.

With our son off to college in pursuit of academic excellence and other college-related rituals, our daughter, a high school senior, decided to take a last-gasp worship-the-sun fling to Florida with some pals before the responsibilities of school and the college search begin.

This left me and my wife HOME ALONE!

The first results from this recent unexpected development are in and I would say this situation is on a scale between blissfully wonderful and downright terrifying.

Just me and Mom, the moment we've been waiting for. No doors to pop open unexpectedly. No 3 a.m. arrivals from a concert. Nobody to worry about getting home safely. No car doors slamming at weird hours. No trail of clothes and shoes from front door to bedroom. No pile of wet towels in the bathroom. The never-ending phone calls suddenly ground to a halt, the opportunities and fantasies suddenly become endless.

Think of dimming the lights, popping open a couple of cold longnecks together, putting on the Cubs game, propping your feet up on the table and ordering a takeout pepperoni and anchovy pizza.

Just kidding.

What I meant to say was: Think of dimming the lights, pushing the furniture to one side of the room, putting a little passionate music on the CD player, popping open a bottle of fine champagne, then having a dance or two . . . and letting things develop from there.

However, neither scenario played out. Instead we did what most normal, functional, happily married couples given this unique opportunity would do:

We cleaned the house from front to back. Vacuumed rugs. Mopped floors. Scrubbed bathtubs. Hung new shower curtains. Scoured toilets. Washed sheets and pillowcases. Threw out trash. Changed light bulbs. Dusted and polished furniture long neglected until we were near exhaustion.

Lord, we even did baseboards and bookshelves. We cleaned out the fish tank. Wait – we don't have a fish tank. It must have been the freezer. I did mention we were exhausted, didn't I?

Chalk it up to nervous energy, that's what we chalked it up to. Chalk it up to the nesting syndrome. Cleaning is therapeutic, someone once said. You can't screw up. What can go wrong – you scrub too much? Put a few more scratches on a tub that is already scratched?

Thrust into this newfound freedom, we didn't know how to react. You know, when for the past 19 years you have lived your lives vicariously through birthday parties, dance recitals, school plays, Little League baseball, homework, science projects, report cards and teacher conferences, Sweet 16 parties, varsity sports, summer camps and summer jobs, dances, dating, non-stop washing of clothes, cooking and cleaning and making lunches, teen-age telephone tag, and the natural progression of events that lead children into adulthood, most parents are so actively involved in their children's activities that they never consciously sit down and plan for this drastic lifestyle change.

At least we obviously didn't.

After a week's preview of the future, the realization has set in that there is going to be time to do all the things we wanted to do but never had the time for.

The question is: What were they?

Bring the photo albums up to date? I don't think so. Plan for retirement? Nope – that's an exercise in futility until college tuitions are over. Clean the garage? We don't have one. Edit the videotapes I've recorded on the camcorder through the years? Probably not.

Like many couples, we were married for several years before we had children. I know we didn't go to kiddie parties and Little League games then, so what did we do?

We did what? Romantic dinners? Great conversations? We bared our souls? We partied all night?

No, no way. That was someone else.

Here's what I foresee happening:

The cat will get a lot of attention. In fact, this cat will be so adored, he may have to go to a cat shrink because he's being smothered with affection.

We probably won't be the first husband-wife team in my fantasy baseball league, but I know my wife will provide some keen insights and support on draft night.

One summer we'll try to hit every major league baseball stadium in the country. That's always been one of her dreams.

But if we do, that would set me up for a lifetime of SweetArts balls, art gallery openings and wine tastings. Well, there are worse things.

Such as?

Poetry readings without alcohol.

Actually, I think we're going to do fine. I haven't broken the news to her yet that I'm interested in joining the NASCAR circuit, but for years she's said it might be fun for a while to live in the fast lane.

To this point all that's ever meant was bowling on an alley that was over-oiled.

Maybe things will change.

I Can't Understand Pillow Talk

February 18, 2000

I shop for new pillows almost as often as some women shop for shoes. It's not that I'm a pillow-aholic and crave the latest styles and trends in pillows — that's not it at all. I hate to shop. The male pillow version of Imelda Marcos I'm not. The problem is this: I destroy pillows.

I don't know what goes on in my bed at night – I've never put an overhead camera in the bedroom. But apparently at some point when I'm snuggled in and traveling through dreamland with the turmoil and chaos of the day far behind me, I must get aggressive. Maybe I think I'm in the ring with Ali or perhaps Hulk Hogan because I pound and wrestle pillows into submission.

The latest pillow to go down for the count lasted about three months. It was not a pretty sight: feathers leaking everywhere, once-proud goose down all over the linens and the floor, and me headed, once again, for the pillow store.

Now this may seem like a simple task to you, but it is far from it to me. To begin with, I am overwhelmed and intimidated by the number of pillows from which to choose. They come in different shapes and sizes, obviously including standard, queen and king. But they also have different fillings, such as goose down, white goose down, power down, poly-down, duck feathers, foam, synthetic whatevers, non-allergenic models and combinations too numerous to mention. Some companies even tout their pillows as overstuffed, like sandwiches.

Every pillow has a sales pitch. One label even said, "There are good pillows . . . and bad pillows." No kidding. So what do you do? You wander around through pillowland, like a lost ball in high weeds, moving from label to label, pulling pillows out of the rack, squeezing them a little, thinking what they might feel like under your head, but really not having a clue because there's no way of knowing unless the pillow spends a couple of nights with you.

I eliminate every pillow that I can't control. If a pillow fights back and doesn't accept the shape I squeeze it into, it's not for me. I have to dominate the pillow. Foam is fine in beer, but not pillows.

So what eventually happens? A couple of squeezes, some basic indecision, a little anxiety and then I make the call. Will it be a good call or a bad one? Only time will tell.

It's always struck me as strange how little time we spend selecting the stuff we spend a third of our lives with. Think about it: You go to buy a mattress, something you're going to sleep on for 15, maybe 20 years, eight hours a night typically, maybe more. How much time do you spend testing it out? Two minutes, tops?

This is the thing in your life that probably means more to your well-being than your home or your car – your mattress. If you don't sleep well, you're cranky, irritable, you don't have any energy, you're bummed out. Yet you walk into a store, check out some labels that say primo power posture whatever or super ultra perfect sleeper – or maybe it tells you that there are more coils per square inch than whatever – as if that's supposed to mean something to you. I mean, who keeps abreast of mattress coil statistics?

Then fully dressed, you self-consciously lie on a couple of mattresses without linens or pillows in the middle of a store with other customers and sales personnel looking at you. "How's that feel?" someone asks.

"Well, it feels like I'm a big dummy lying in bed with my clothes on in the middle of a store." You do this for maybe a minute or two, bounding from mattress to mattress and then, out of frustration, make a decision.

Can you imagine walking into a car dealership and sitting in the driver's seat of a couple of models for two minutes, checking out the upholstery and saying, "I'll take that"? Of course not. At a reputable dealership, you'd get to road test a demo car for a few hours, maybe even a day or two.

But you spend more time in your bed with your pillow than any other place in the house and way more time than you spend in your car each day, and how much time do you take to buy a mattress and pillow? Ten minutes combined? Fifteen?

It seems as if every time I went to buy a mattress, I had the thought driven into me that it had to be extra firm, because extra firm is good for your back. Yet it seems that whenever I stay in some goat farm motel in Goatsville in the middle of nowhere, the mattress is soft and cheap and there's not much to it – and I sleep like a baby. And wonder why I didn't buy a super soft squishy mattress.

So what's the moral to this story? Absolutely none. Some stories don't have a moral – or a point — you should know that by now. Some stories just ramble.

By the way, the pillow I purchased had a picture of a bulldozer running over a pillow. The name of it was "The Uncrushable Pillow."

We'll see.

Free of Grass, Free at Last

August 11, 2000

I was brought up in the money-can't-buy-happiness school, taught to be thankful for the little things in life, not to expect big things such as wealth and riches, mansions and servants, but if they came my way, that would simply be an unexpected bonus.

Well, the ship has yet to come in but it turns out that the little things are the most important anyway – good friends and good times, a couple of nice kids who made it through college, a wife that puts up with my shenanigans and can cook, good health, a decent round of golf once or twice a year, an occasional trifecta that hits, a cold beer on a hot day, an afternoon at Wrigley Field, a steak burnt on the outside but red in the middle – those sorts of things.

Well, the other morning I was taking a walk and realized I had something else to be thankful for – something I hadn't thought about in a while. I saw a guy pushing a lawnmower in grass that looked to be a foot high. His face was florid, he was sweating buckets, and he was not halfway finished. I did some quick math and

187

realized that I had not touched a lawnmower in 14 years – simply because I have no grass to cut.

When we moved into the house we live in now in 1986 there was a back yard with a carpet of St. Aug on it. I took one look at it and did not think, well, what should it be — a new Snapper? A Toro? A Briggs & Stratton? No, I did not think any of those. I did not even think Poulan Weed-Eater. I thought one thing and one thing only:

Bricks.

By that time in my life, I had evolved from a person who was once a cultivator and admirer of grass into someone who hated to cut grass, absolutely loathed it, and I will explain that transformation momentarily.

So I dug up the grass, leveled the dirt, had a couple of pallets of old red delivered, painstakingly laid them and – Voila! – instant patio. At the time the house was being painted. My cranky old lawnmower that made the move from our old house I offered to the painter, and he took it. Ever since that day, we have had a bricked-in yard surrounded by a low-maintenance garden that is headquarters for barbecuing, hanging out when the weather is decent and admiring the flowers.

And for that I am very, very thankful.

Bricks, I should add, are pretty easy to take care of. Every once in a while a couple of weeds pop up between the cracks but you just get out the weed-zapper and spray them.

Now I know there are people who make their living cutting grass and to them I say, bless you. And I have friends who have so much grass that they have a riding lawnmower, who claim that there is nothing more relaxing than climbing on top of the old John Deere and getting after it. To them I say, yes, there is something more relaxing than that:

It's slouching on a sofa inside an air-conditioned house looking out at a bricked-in patio.

Allow me to explain where I'm coming from. Growing up, my father was a grass-cutting fool. Before power mowers, he got after it with a push mower. Before power edgers, he did it with a hand sickle. No complaints, ever. It was his passion to keep the yard meticulously neat and trimmed, like someone who gets frequent haircuts. And when he finally purchased his first power mower, you'd have thought we had bought a Cadillac Coupe De Ville.

No lawnmower has ever been treated so well, ever been so maintained and adored. That was his thing and that was the mentality I was brought up in: Cutting and edging grass is a passion, a love affair. One other thing I should mention: We did not have that much grass and I always yearned for more.

So, when my wife and I moved for a few years from Uptown, where yards are relatively small, we found ourselves in Bucktown, where yards are considerably larger. Actually, we were in Buck Vista, Bucktown purists would correct, but that's not the point. Finally, I thought to myself, I had just what I always wanted – a large yard of lush green grass I could cultivate and fertilize and cut and trim to my heart's content, where the kids could romp around and play and we could sit around and talk about how pretty the grass was.

Well, the grass in Bucktown is so lush and fertile, it hardly needs fertilizer. I had never been around a yard like this. You cut it one day, it seemed, and by the time you finished bagging up the clippings, the first section you cut had already started growing.

Oh well, I thought, I'll cut it religiously once a week. Wrong. If you let it go a week or more than a week, you had to cut it twice. You had to raise the mower to its highest level because it couldn't get through the tall grass, then cut it, then lower the blades and cut it again. In the summertime, which lasts approximately nine months in New Orleans, I cut it once every four days.

Or so it seemed.

The novelty of having a beautiful manicured yard wore off quickly. By the time I had recovered from the dreaded ordeal of cranking up the mower, it was time to face the music again. I fully realized that I had not inherited my dad's grass-cutting genes. By the time we moved out, I was praying for hard freezes, droughts, cinch bugs and plagues of locusts.

None of those happened, of course. But in a grass-free homestead, I became a new man. And for years, every time I drove by

Carrollton Lumber & Wrecking Co., and saw those pallets of bricks stacked up, I said thank you, Lord. Free of grass, free at last.

Color Me Confused

September 6, 2006

As the damage to our ceilings and walls is finally being repaired and re-Sheetrocked, we have gotten to the really, really fun stage of picking out paint colors.

Next to a husband and wife wallpapering a bathroom together, it's as delightful an experience as there is for a couple.

Needless to say, my wife is so lucky to have my expertise on selecting and coordinating colors. I hesitate to say she's ecstatic about my tastes, but I know she appreciates and values my opinions and assistance.

Just the other day, for example, she asked me what I thought might be a good color to repaint the kitchen and the den it flows into. I had just gotten out of the shower and I held up the wet kinda raspberry-colored wash cloth I had used and said, "How about this?"

I got "the look."

I took the wash cloth to the paint wheel and flipped through it. It matched up perfectly with the shade called Cinco de Mayo.

"Look – it would be perfect for a party," I said. "Think of the room as our canvas and we are the artists. We could get some piñatas that matched, add some sombreros and serapes, pull it all together with some samba music and Jose Cuervo. I know how you love theme parties, so every year on Cinco de Mayo . . . whaddya think?"

Dead silence.

"Hey, there's two more colors that might work, Picante and Habanero Pepper. We could do the Macarena."

I have a gut feeling the kitchen is not going to be Cinco de

Mayo. But not far removed from that color on the wheel was a much lighter version of it, a very nice and tempting color named Tippy Toes. It may be a fine color but my den where I watch ESPN is NOT going to be painted Tippy Toes.

The color wheel's instructions say it "is designed for easy color selection and is intended for use by architects, designers and painting contractors."

What – they forgot columnists?

In the early selection stages, my wife said she might be leaning toward some sort of khaki for the trim on the outside of the house, which is also being painted. "Go in my closet – you ought to be able to find something in there. I got every color imaginable," I said. Except for a very few suits and a blazer, my whole wardrobe is khaki pants and chinos.

Actually, she looked.

In my next life, I want to be the guy who selects names for colors of paint. It might not pay much but it sure could be kicks. If someone is going to buy a color named Squirrel Tail or Snugglepuss (which I am not making up; it's a terrible shade of purple) chances are he or she might go for Octopus or Road Carrion — or maybe even Bus Exhaust.

My wife brought home some samples for one bathroom. We were looking at blues and greens or a combination of those colors. I picked out an aqua that matched the color of my shampoo, which comes in an opaque bottle. The shampoo is named Ocean Breeze.

We painted the bathroom that color, which should have been named Electric Turquoise. Moral: Never select paint by matching it to shampoo.

Another color was actually named Old Pickup Blue. Conjures up a great image, doesn't it? Was it a rusted-out Ford? A beat-up Chevy on cinder blocks?

There's also a deeper blue named Grandma's Sweater. Maybe it comes with some moth holes in it. Then there's a more aqua blue named House of Blues, a grayer blue named I've Got the Blues and I guess a more azure blue named Un-teal We Meet Again.

You look at these colors so long until you can't tell blue from green. The outside of the house is being painted Covington Blue, which looks green and I suspect has nothing to do with the city north of the lake. There's also a North Shore Green, but then again, there's a lot of north shores in this country.

We painted the trim on the outside Montgomery White. It is not white – it is cream, deep cream – nothing white about it.

"What do you think about this color for a bedroom?" she said, pointing to Soft Fern.

"Mmmmmm," I said.

"What about this one?"

"Mmmmmm, maybe."

Those "Mmmmms" are not what she wanted to hear, I'm pretty sure.

Problem is, the swatches on the wheel are 1 inch by 2 inches and you hold that up against a wall that is 18 feet long and 12 feet high and well, unless you're clairvoyant it's really hard to tell what a whole wall of Old Straw Hat or Baby Turtle (yes, there really is) will look like.

So, my wife goes to the paint store and buys quart samples of paint at $11 a pop and before you know it, we have so many quarts of paint we don't like and will never use, we could have done filets and fine red wine at any top 10 restaurant in the city for the money we spent.

I say dump 'em all in a bucket, mix it up and agree to paint a room with it, no matter the color. Call it Roll the Dice.

I'm game.

A Letter From Mrs. Angus Lind

November 1, 1982

Dear Drs. Masters and Johnson, Steincrohn, Mendelsohn and Joyce Brothers:

I have a headache. A grinding, agonizing, persistent, ever-present cerebral throb.

I'm writing to all of you about this because I'm not sure whether it's physical, psychological or just likely to influence my sex life.

The pain comes – in the afternoons – and goes – in the mornings. It usually stays with me all day on weekends, except on sunny Saturdays and Sundays perfect for viewing or pursuing outdoor sports.

It hovers on the fringes of my well-being when I hear the pop of the top of a can of Dixie, and creases my brow when "The Star-Spangled Banner" heralds yet another evening of games with the boob . . . er, on the tube.

It pounds like the hooves of hundreds of horses when the track opens each fall. But it is most excruciating when The Times-Picayune is delivered at dawn on Mondays, Wednesdays and Fridays.

Anxiously I turn to the Living Section to see if the headache has struck again. Sometimes I am spared. The victims of the alleged witticisms running down the left-hand column of the section cover are the Superdome concessionaires, women's libbers, our state legislators.

But more often, gentle readers, I am the victim. The headache is mine.

He's tall, blond, and occasionally well hung . . . over. He's an armchair jock, a Tulane fan whose outpourings of devotion to his alma mater are guaranteed to turn anyone green, a friend of the common man (and the commoner the better), a self-proclaimed expert on women.

And he's more chauvinistic than Bob Greene or Mike Royko, with whom he shares the indistinction of being a newspaper columnist. His frequent broadsides against the better sex do bring home the bacon, doctors, but I wind up smeared with the grease.

He's Woodward and Bernstein in one inquisitive body when it comes to investigative reporting, but he doesn't roam the corridors of the Capitol or probe the recesses of parking garages. He's more likely to be found in our bathroom, musing about the cosmic problem of why I put the toilet paper roll on backwards or pillaging the medicine cabinet to develop a scintillating column on the number of beauty aids I need to be the 10 he wants.

Or, he's in the kitchen critiquing culinary arts, which he seldom practices himself, and complaining that I can't make hamburger taste like Beef Wellington.

The results of these homefront fact-finding missions, dear doctors, always get into print, leaving me with egg on my face and his readers with grins on theirs.

Then, when he has a case of writer's block, he strives for the unique. How about a column on August and what's wrong with it? There's nothing so unlovely as an August day, he penned, especially the one we were married on. Our anniversary dinner this year was an especially merry one.

Fancying himself as a closet financial analyst, he tackled the budget. But not the national one – oh, no – ours. He discussed my balancing act as though it were a three-ring circus and I taught the three R's for years knowing that my pupils' parents were chortling over my well-publicized ignorance of one of them.

Not content with these crimes against marriage, this aggressive journalist turned purse snatcher. The result: an amusing little piece about what women carry in them, and my private life was out of my handbag forever.

But nothing is sacred when you're the wife of the national enquirer. Carol Burnett can sue and win when maligned, but I must keep smiling even when I'm approaching motherhood and am lovingly described in print as "a beached whale" because I can't get up off the sofa.

You can see that the agony has become chronic, doctors, so what I want to know is this:

Should I take a pill for my headache, give a pill to my headache, or figure out a way to get rid of that big-mouthed pill altogether?

— Sincerely, Mrs. Angus Lind

CHAPTER 12
Lagniappe

St. Henry's: Ignatius J. Reilly's Church

August 1, 2007

Originally established in 1856 to meet the needs of a large German immigrant community in Uptown New Orleans, the Church of St. Henry is one of God's special places overseen by a jovial German priest whose joyful spirit never flags.

The church, located on Gen. Pershing right off Magazine Street, is celebrating its 150th anniversary. It is as N'Awlins as it gets and is significant for a variety of reasons.

One of the most intriguing and amusing attributes is that it is the church to which the mother of the slovenly Ignatius J. Reilly forced him to accompany her to Mass in "Confederacy of Dunces." Forcing the rebellious Ignatius to Mass was not a good idea.

"He had collapsed twice on the way to the church and had collapsed once again during the sermon about sloth, reeling out of the pew and creating an embarrassing disturbance," wrote John Kennedy Toole in his hilarious Pulitzer Prize-winning novel, which is also as New Orleans as it gets.

Msgr. Henry H. Engelbrecht, known to all as "Father Henry," came to the church to be its pastor in 1990 and immediately embraced it.

"I fell in love with the place from the very beginning. It's so uniquely New Orleans. Those people in the 'Confederacy of Dunces' – they're still here," the 65-year-old clergyman said.

As if the exclamation point needed to be dotted again, fancy this: The church is named St. Henry's. The pastor is named Henry.

There's a deacon named Henry, Henry Garon, a retired Loyola physics professor. The church custodian is a Henry, Henry Jobin, making a good argument that this is a "Confederacy of Henrys."

In his current best-seller, "The Joy of Y'at Catholicism," author Earl Higgins calls Father Henry "a joyous Y'at" who invites some friends to the rectory for an all-day Bacchus party that starts around noon the Sunday before Mardi Gras and ends when the last Bacchus float passes by.

"We call it Thoth Sunday now," said Father Henry. "I made a mistake by calling it Bacchus Sunday at first, because we have another fine parade called Thoth that same day." Not to mention that four past kings of Thoth attend St. Henry's services. At morning Mass before the party, the congregation sings, as is the tradition on the Sunday before Mardi Gras, "If Ever I Cease to Love."

Mass is enjoyable, say those who attend, because of the good father's ability to make them listen through his sense of humor.

"I like to tell stories because that's the way Jesus taught," Father Henry said, "only they were called parables. They might not remember what you said but they'll remember the story and relate it to what Jesus said.

"You're supposed to make the word of God relevant to people, and if you don't reach those people, what's the point?"

The priest's humorous take on life is obvious in casual conversation. Referring to his own use of crutches and a wheelchair to get around and talking about the church's longtime organist, Francis Matherne, who is blind, Father Henry said, "If I'm on crutches and we go somewhere together, he'll put his hand on my shoulder and I'll lead him. It's quite a sight."

The 18th Feast of St. Henry Annual Reunion, part of the sesquicentennial celebration, was held recently.

Even in a regular year, the reunion, Father Henry said, "brings back people from all over the city – we pack 'em in," he said. "The people love this parish, they're workers and they will fight for this parish – it's amazing."

The criteria for the reunion are, not surprisingly, humorous: You're part of St. Henry's if you went to school there (the parish school closed in 1973). Or if you go to church there regularly, or if you who ever lived in the parish, or if you ever went to church there, or if you're named Henry, or if you know someone named Henry. So it's practically anybody who ever drove by.

"The people who come have a great love for this parish. It never ceases to amaze me," the priest said.

Coming in to celebrate this year was Bishop Roger Morin. He was introduced as someone who came to St. Henry's as a seminarian, studying to become an ordained priest. He then became Deacon Roger, then Father Morin as assistant pastor, then pastor, and now auxiliary bishop of the Archdiocese of New Orleans.

At which point one of the St. Henry parishioners wisecracked, "This guy can't keep a job."

Remember, it is the church in "Confederacy of Dunces."

St. Henry's once boasted what one parishioner called "a really jumpin' CYO program." CYO dances were strong citywide but nowhere were they stronger than St. Henry's, where the featured attractions were Irma Thomas, Ernie K-Doe and Oliver "Who Shot the La-La" Morgan. There was also a boxing program and sports teams.

On Saturday the church will host a "CYO Reunion Dance" in the old school auditorium at 821 Gen. Pershing featuring Benny Grunch and the Bunch. Knowing some of the St. Henry's alums, in their honor, and tongue-in-cheek, Grunch has written a "GED Fight Song."

Despite the GED humor, St. Henry's has turned out some fine scholars and big-name athletes, including Johnny Arthurs, who starred at basketball for Tulane University and went on to play for the Milwaukee Bucks; Frank Wills, who pitched for Tulane and played for the Kansas City Royals; and Marty Wetzel, a Tulane linebacker who played for the New York Jets.

Father Henry grew up on Marengo Street near Freret in Our Lady of Lourdes Parish. His dad was a Lutheran, his mom a Catholic. He went to school there and then on to Jesuit, although loyal St. Henry's grads who largely went to Redemptorist High tell the good father he should do some revisionist history on his resume and claim Redemptorist as his school of record.

"That's the way it is here, people say that kind of stuff to me," he said. "We're like a family. Everybody knows everybody's business and what we don't know we make up. We've got third, fourth and fifth generations here. Geographically it's small but in spirit it's huge."

Like many churches, although its demographics have changed, St. Henry's is a survivor – it has adapted to different circumstances, different times and different needs.

The history of the parish could easily be entitled "Against All Odds," which was a phrase used by Father Henry's classmate, Bishop Robert Muench of Baton Rouge, at the feast celebration in 2006. Today the former parish school is being put to good use as it houses an Orleans Parish public school and the school annex building is home for El Yo Yo Day Care.

In another twist of irony, a short block away at Napoleon and Magazine is a neighborhood tavern named Mrs. Mae's, which was once named Engelbracht's Beer Parlor, just a vowel removed from the current pastor's name. It was owned by – get this – Henry (what else?) and Albert Engelbracht.

With a number of German pastors, it fit that the church was located on Berlin Street. (The largest street in that area was named Napoleon Avenue. Then came Berlin, Milan, Marengo, Constantinople and Austerlitz streets – named for Napoleon's great conquests.)

Berlin Street was changed to General Pershing during World War I when this country was at war with Germany.

"Berlin was not a street you wanted to live on then," said Father Henry, who would like to see it changed back because of the German heritage of the neighborhood and because No. 74, the old address of the rectory on Berlin Street, can still be found in ceramic tile in the pavement outside it.

After Katrina, Father Henry and Monsignor Ignatius Roppolo were able to return to the parish the first weekend in October.

"We got back October 1st and had Mass that weekend. We didn't announce it, people just showed up," Father Henry said. About

40 attended.

The next week a wedding was planned. It was touch and go. Father Henry decided to hit the go button, and married Jaimie Dill and Jason Ledet. The national media reported the wedding.

"I'm really proud of that," he said. "It was probably the first wedding celebrated on the East Bank of the city (after the storm). And I've already baptized their first baby."

A fallen pecan tree had to be removed from the roof of the church and some temporary repairs were made. The following weekend a full schedule of Masses were held in church.

"He was hell-bent or should I say heaven-bent on re-opening this parish," said parishioner Alden Hagardorn, pastoral council president. "That's what makes this place so special."

Not so fast, my friend, said Father Henry. "It's the people, not me. They love this church. Now I love New Orleans. And I love being stationed in New Orleans. It's wonderful to be a pastor in your own hometown, a place which has been described as America's most interesting city. That's a hard combination to beat.

"And this is simply a lovely little church."

(Sadly, St. Henry's was ultimately closed by the Archdiocese of New Orleans. Parishioners have waged an on-going battle to have it re-opened.)

War Story:
Cologne & Paratrooper Philip M. Hannan

July 13, 1980

When a young German priest named Friedhelm Hofman was about to become canon of the historic Cathedral of Cologne in West Germany, old Canon Kleff sat him down and told him there were some things he must know about the cathedral that no one else knew.

The largest Gothic church in northern Europe is situated in the heart of Cologne, a large river port on the Rhine. It is a classic in German Gothic architecture, begun in 1248 and completed in 1880. Its great twin towers dominate the city, rising 516 feet into the sky. Its 14th-century stained glass choir windows are some of the most beautiful in the world. And the church's works of art – its relics, chalice and statues, and the Shrine of the Magi – are priceless.

Cologne, being a river port and key transportation route, was ripped apart by 262 Allied air raids. There were 20,000 casualties. A population nearing one million at one point had shrunk to 69,000 by April, 1945. Ninety-one of Cologne's 150 churches had somehow survived with only medium damage.

But this was not what Kleff wanted to tell the young canon about. He wanted to tell him the story of how a young American Catholic chaplain saved the church's treasures from pillage: The chaplain took it on himself to cross security lines to have himself named temporary pastor of the church so the treasures could be guarded from looters and more bombardment during the close of World War II.

Hofman listened attentively as the old canon told how the young American found him hiding in the basement of the church, trying to protect the valuables by himself. Then how the chaplain got permission to take charge of the church until the military government took over.

The Germans being the good record keepers they are, the American priest's name was recorded on a document. It was Capt. Philip M. Hannan, USA, of the 505th Parachute Regiment of the 82nd Airborne Division. Hofman filed the story away in his memory.

Three years ago, Sister Andre Becker, O.S.U., a member of the Ursuline community of New Orleans, visited Cologne and met Hofman. They talked about the priest from New Orleans, and Hofman was surprised to learn that he is now the Archbishop of New Orleans. The two toured a castle together; the sister thanked him for his hospitality, and she told him she would love to show him New Orleans if he ever got over here.

"Some day I will," he promised.

Last week, "some day" happened. Thirty-six years after the incident at Cologne, Friedhelm Hofman, Canon of the Cathedral of Cologne, stood in Archbishop Philip M. Hannan's office on Walmsley Avenue and warmly presented him with a book about the Cathedral of Cologne. Inscribed in it is: "With heartful greetings and thanks for all you have done during the end of the war. Friedhelm Hofman, Canon of the Cathedral of Cologne."

To say the least, Hannan was stunned that a chapter from his past had come back to him on such a nice note.

The archbishop sat down and relived what happened. He had visited the cathedral before the war in 1938 when he was a student at Rome. So he was more than familiar with the value of the treasures in the church when the Allied forces took Cologne.

"I almost got killed trying to get in the cathedral," said the archbishop, who is prone to modestly understating his accomplishments, including his paratroop jumps. "The Germans across the river had a good field of fire. I jumped from one bit of rubble to another and finally got there.

"A priest came up from the cellar. He was Canon Kleff, and he is still alive today. He had been asked to stay there and guard the cathedral. When I saw him, he had dust all over him. I realized that in time of war, you need more than one priest to stand up and say, 'You can't come in here.'"

The treasures had been placed in specially-built bunkers inside the cathedral. They were made of masonry and shaped like igloos. But Hannan said a simple grenade could have blown them apart. So he broke the security lines and found his archbishop. He convinced him that what he wanted to do was the right thing. The archbishop authorized him to take charge and appointed him pastor.

"I stationed a guard at the cathedral to keep anybody from blowing up the bunkers. I also told the paratroopers that if they had taken anything at all from the cathedral as a souvenir to return it to me . . . and all of them did," he laughed.

"Cologne was devastated," Hannan said. "On our flank was an American infantry division, but I didn't know anybody in it. I didn't know if they realized the value of these art treasures. The German people were starving and they would do anything at this point."

So the guards stayed until the military government arrived and took over about two weeks later. "The link is," said Hannan, "that Canon Kleff remembered that I came there and passed it on."

"The treasures are still there today, some in their old places," beamed Canon Hofman. "They are still there for all to see.

"Some good things happened after the war," he said. "Excavations were begun, and three other cathedrals were found – one built in 870, one built in 560 and one built in 320. Even a Roman temple from 15 A.D. was uncovered."

In 1981, the cathedral's appearance is marred by crumbling stone, a problem made worse by pollution in the air.

It will take decades to carefully replace the destroyed parts. So large is the structure, which seats 18,000, that there is still unrepaired war damage.

Remodeling and construction is a permanent part of the décor, so much so that it can safely be predicted that no one living today will ever see the cathedral without scaffolding. There is a saying in Cologne: "When the cathedral is completed, the world will end."

Still, the treasures are intact, thanks to the actions of a Catholic chaplain from New Orleans.

Every Man a King

January 20, 1978

On a cold rainy night in the winter of 1934, about this time of the year, Blue Room orchestra leader Castro Carazo was putting on his tuxedo, getting ready for his first show of the night when the phone in his room rang.

"Castro, I want you to come over here right away," the voice said. "Seymour already has a car waiting for you in front of the hotel." Calling from Baton Rouge was Sen. Huey P. Long. Seymour was Seymour Weiss, owner of the Roosevelt Hotel.

"Everything was 'right away' or 'right now' with Huey," Professor Carazo, now 82, recalled this week at his Baton Rouge studio. "When we got to the senator's apartment on the eighth floor of the old Heidelberg (hotel), we were met by two bodyguards. That wasn't unusual, though. What was unusual was that the senator was asleep. It was the only time during our friendship that I ever saw him snoozing, catnapping a little bit.

"He was a living dynamo, worked day and night, never slept much," the professor said.

So Carazo went to bed but not for long. About 3 a.m. Huey came into his room, shook him and said, "Get up, Castro. We have plenty work to do. You know I'm going to run for the presidency in 1936, don't you?" the Kingfish asked.

"Yes, I've heard all that," the musician replied.

"Well, I need a campaign song, and we're going to do it right now," Long said. So Carazo got some hotel stationery, and lined off some staffs, while Long perused the morning papers and drank coffee.

"It wasn't that long a time that a little melody came to my mind," the native of San Jose, Costa Rica, recalled. "I followed all the rules – not too high, not too low, a simple key." About 25 minutes later, Carazo said, "Senator, I have it."

"Whistle it for me," Huey said. Carazo did.

"Damn good," Long said, "damn good. Now hand me a pad and pencil and whistle it again. Now the second line."

About a half hour later, the old maestro recalled, Long had the words. It was getting near dawn, and there were about 15 people standing outside his suite waiting to see him. Long opened the door wearing his pajamas and slippers and said, "Com'on in, boys, you're going to hear my song for the first time!" Within half an hour, the reporters, cronies, and friends were all standing around Long's baby grand piano, with Carazo at the keyboard, singing the song that has become a Louisiana legend: "Every Man a King."

Why weep or slumber, America
Land of brave and true
With castles, clothing and food for all;
All belongs to you.
Ev'ry man a king. Ev'ry man a king
For you can be a millionaire
But there's something belonging to others
There's enough for all people to share;
When it's sunny June and December too,
Or in the winter time or spring,
There'll be peace without end,
Every neighbor a friend,
With ev'ry man a king.

Today at the Chateau Capitol (the old Heidelberg), on the 50th anniversary of Long's election as governor, Carazo is being honored and a plaque will be placed in the room in which the song was composed. The professor will play the song on the very same piano he played it on at the hotel. "I sent a piano tuner over," he laughed. "I was worried about what might come out of it."

Carazo studied at the Royal Conservatory of Music at Barcelona, Spain for four years. He went back to Costa Rica because of his dad's poor health, and after he died, he went to New York where he was directing an orchestra on Flatbush Avenue in Brooklyn. There he met E.V. Richards Jr., who asked Carazo to come to New Orleans to open up his recently-purchased Saenger Theater.

So in 1927, there was Castro Carazo and his orchestra of 35 sharing top billing with Douglas Fairbanks and Mary Pickford in "The Gaucho." Some years later, after he "sent in my resignations three times," Carazo left. Then after a year back in Costa Rica, he and his wife from Abbeville found themselves back in New Orleans, with Carazo opening up Seymour Weiss' Blue Room.

He met the Kingfish, who had an apartment on the third floor, one afternoon when his orchestra was practicing. Long pulled up a chair next to the bandleader and told him about a song called

"Smoke Gets in Your Eyes" that he had heard in New York. Unable to find it in his stack of about 750 numbers, Carazo and Long went upstairs to Carazo's room where Long shuffled through more stacks of orchestrations until he found it.

They they went back to the Blue Room, and after a warmup, Carazo invited Long to direct the orchestra, handed him his stick, and stepped down. A frustrated musician who loved music, Long "was in seventh heaven, with his big eyes just looking at the ceiling." From that point, a very close friendship was born.

So close, that when the time came, the Kingfish made another call to Carazo at the Roosevelt just before curtain call. "Didn't you know you were fired this afternoon?" Long asked.

"He never asked me if I wanted to live in Baton Rouge, never told me what my salary was – those were all minor details to be worked out later on." Once again, a big black Cadillac limo pulled up in front of the hotel, and Carazo found himself once again grabbing a few hours of sleep at Long's apartment. This time, Huey woke him up at 2 a.m. and ordered him to call Dr. James Smith, president of LSU, and then Maj. Troy Middleton, and tell them to be in the governor's office at 3:30 a.m.

When Long and Carazo got to the Capitol about 3:15 a.m., Gov. O.K. Allen was already there. "He told Allen to move over, get out of his chair," Carazo recalled. "He put his feet up on that beautiful desk." Then, when Smith and Middleton arrived, he informed them that Carazo was the new director of bands, and was to get anything he wanted – scholarships, uniforms, money – and was to answer only to Long. "It was a heck of a way of doing business," the professor said, "but that's the way he was."

At LSU from 1934 to 1940, Carazo turned what was once a small military band into a marching showpiece. He wrote many of LSU's fight songs, and Huey added the words. Since 1940, he has taught privately.

On Sept. 10, 1935, mortally wounded by an assassin's bullet two days earlier, Huey Long's dreams for the presidency came to an end at Our Lady of the Lake Hospital. About a hour and a half before he was shot, in the marble hallway of the Capitol, Carazo had been in his office, talking about a dream of his own, a school of music in New Orleans.

"He told me, 'Castro, we're going to go through with it. And we're going to get the money for it from the oil companies. We'll talk about it some more.'"

"My wife should be here, senator," Carazo said. "I'll be seeing you," were his last words to Long.

Carazo learned the news a few hours later. He went to the hospital, where a surgeon told him the senator wasn't going to make it. Carazo went home and began to compose a funeral march for his beloved friend. "I guess we musicians express ourselves with music," he said. The funeral was set for noon, and the band rehearsed the song for the first time at 9 a.m.

"There must have been a hundred thousand people there, but they were silent, except for those who were crying," Carazo said.

Arguments still rage in Louisiana and the rest of the country over whether the Kingfish was a friend or enemy of the people of Louisiana, and whether his wealth-sharing philosophy, as reflected in his campaign song, could become a reality.

"His campaign was rolling," Carazo said. "The unions were for Huey Long, all that share the wealth stuff. I don't know how he was going to do it, but he sure wanted to even things up. What I like to remember about him is that he was tough, but he was kind. I liked his ways, liked to be with him. He was a great fellow.

"I sure have missed him."

How Sarge Donnels Got Conned

October 24, 2006

Sixty-one years ago, the Detroit Tigers, led by Hammerin' Hank Greenberg, met the Chicago Cubs in the last World Series played during World War II.

Greenberg, who almost caught Babe Ruth in 1938 with 58

home runs, had lost four years serving his country overseas. The future Hall of Famer returned to the team midway through the 1945 season and led his team to the American League pennant.

The Cubs, behind the pitching arm of Hank Borowy, were looking for their third Series win, the first two coming in 1907 and '08 against, ironically, the same Detroit Tigers who are the Cinderella story of this year's World Series with the St. Louis Cardinals.

It would be the Cubs' last appearance in the World Series, a sad story without an uplifting chapter in the foreseeable future.

Sixty-one years ago, while waiting to go home after the end of World War II, New Orleanian Johnny Donnels, a first sergeant, and a gang of his soldier buddies in the Fourth Engineer Amphibian Brigade were at the Replacement Depot in Japan, sitting around a makeshift pot-belly stove with freezing temperatures outside . . . waiting to hear the broadcast of the 1945 World Series.

The brigade had been stationed in New Guinea, an important part of the Pacific Theater that led to the liberation of the Philippines from Japanese occupation. They had brought over some 1,200 landing boats, the Higgins boats made here in New Orleans. Standard issue for the troops in New Guinea were machetes, used for the troops to cut their way through the thick jungles where soldiers joked that there were nine months of rain followed by monsoons.

"In New Guinea there was no communication, none," said Donnels, an accomplished professional photographer and artist and a French Quarter icon. "Life Magazine came out and we didn't know it. We didn't know who Sinatra was. When we finally got to hear him, we said, hey, he's got a nice voice, he's gonna go someplace."

So needless to say, Donnels and his pals didn't even know who was playing in the World Series. "We had no idea who won in '44 or '43," he said. "We were incommunicado."

Unbeknownst to the troops, the Army Signal Corps had recorded the game hours earlier, then waited to present it to the base camp at a more reasonable time. "It was such a thrill to get to listen to it,"

Donnels said.

As it turned out, it was the second game of the Series at Briggs Stadium in Detroit, Borowy having shut out the Tigers 9-0 in the first game.

"At a certain point in the game (the fifth inning), a soldier jumped up and shouted, 'Twenty dollars says that Hank Greenberg will hit a home run!'" Donnels recalled.

Well, the soldiers, including Donnels, started pulling out money, thinking this guy was nuts. Now, $20 was a lot of money back in 1945, "but we had a lot of money because where we had been there was no place to spend it and no way to spend it."

"The guy had lots of takers, including this sad-sack," he said.

It was just seconds later when Hammerin' Hank unloaded a three-run home run which would eventually lead to a 4-1 Tigers victory.

"He took us for a lot of $20 bills," Donnels said, recalling the soldiers forking over a lot of money to this one guy. "What we didn't know and it wasn't until later that we found out, was that the GI was with the Signal Corps and knew the result of the game and what was going to happen."

It was a great con, not unlike the plot line of the Paul Newman and Robert Redford movie, "The Sting."

Unfortunately, the Signal Corps was not stationed anywhere near where Donnels and his troops were, so this guy pulled a fast one, hit the road and never got his just due, which would have been a good old-fashioned butt-whuppin'.

After the War, Donnels, a Warren Easton graduate, came home and enrolled in the New Orleans Academy of Art in the French Quarter, vowing that the Army would be his last employer. It went bankrupt and closed a year later, but Donnels persisted with his artwork and did well.

In 1970, he got into photography "by accident. I swapped a couple of paintings for a camera, and well, it's been a pretty nice life."

He's now 82, still productive and sharp, his photos are known worldwide and he can be found regularly in his art and photo studio on St. Peter Street, a block from Pat O'Brien's. It seems as if he's been there forever.

"I'm still enjoying it," he said.

The Greenberg home run story he recalled because the Tigers are in the Series. He sent an email account of the con story to a buddy of his named Paul who sent back this reply:

"Fast forward: I'm in Japan listening to a Chicago Bulls basketball game on the short-wave band of a Sony radio I'd just purchased. Later, after the Bulls won, 102-98, I headed for the hotel bar where they were playing a delayed broadcast of the game.

"Needless to say, I didn't pay for one single drink . . . Same church, different pew."

(Johnny Donnels died in March of 2009. He was 84.)

Tilted Years: Playing the Machines

August 28, 1973

Somewhere in the world, Spittin' Jerry is keeping a close eye on the Jim Garrison pinball bribery trial.

Jerry's world was "tilted" more than two years ago when the feds turned out the lights on the nudies that danced across the odds-boards of Border Beauties and Frisco Cities – and forever silenced the clickety-clickings that were music to his ears.

Jerry was a pro pinball player.

Payoff pinball machines were another chapter in the history of gambling – whether legal or illegal – in New Orleans.

I grew up during that time and I must credit pinball machines with keeping me out of dirty pool halls.

They kept me in dirty barrooms.

So it is with a tear in my eye, a lump in my throat, and the memory of calluses worn like a medal on my hands that I recall the years of my misspent youth – and the characters I met, like Jerry, during a time that apparently will not return.

Pinballs, more popularly known as "playing the machines," was an athletic endeavor, if not a sport. It took a special kind of strong-armed, quick-witted person to conquer the machine, mentally and physically.

Beer-drinking was probably the best conditioner for the game, but weightlifting and staring at the machine were good training aides.

Good players were strong, with well-callused hands and cat-quick reflexes. You could always spot a bad player by the way he flinched when he really jolted a machine. If a hard hit bothered him, his hands weren't tough enough.

Strength wasn't the only prerequisite for the complete player. A pro would have the entire number board memorized so he wouldn't have to worry about checking it during the course of a game to see what numbers were winners. Instead, he could keep his head down and concentrate on following the drop of the pinball and readying for his next hit.

Early pinball boards had 25 numbers and later models only 20. Three numbers in a line or in a section produced a winner.

In one section on an old machine, two numbers in the blue section scored 600 games, but the shot came rarely and was difficult to hit. On some machines, a number placed in each corner of the board also scored 600.

Six hundred games, at the rate of a nickel a game, translated into $30. That was considered a pretty good cash-in.

A good hit into a winning number was always rewarded by comments from professional onlookers who awaited a big score so they could get a free round of beer.

"Nice hit, good biff, you da babe, way to rap it," were considered suitable compliments that would bring a free round for the barflies.

My crowd played the Uptown circuit, a pretty tough league. It was kind of a status symbol to be thrown out of a bar for winning too much. It was like getting ruled off a race track – the management knew you were cheating but couldn't prove it. You were just winning too much, so you were asked to leave. Sometimes we were cheating.

Legends grew quickly in the Uptown league. You could walk around and wait for newcomers to turn their heads and whisper, "See that guy, he's something else. They won't let him play in here."

I wasn't ever asked to leave a bar because I was not a threat to the cash register, but a lot of my friends were.

I was lucky. At best, I was a borderline player, but I hung around with enough good players that some of their skill had to rub off on me. At least I could "go in cow" (pool our money) with them and be able to hold up my half of the play.

Playing pinballs taught me lessons I will carry through life and pass on to my children: It costs a lot of money, they're tough to beat; and you need a good low stance with your feet spread apart to give the machine a really good lick with your hands.

Almost every Friday and Saturday that I didn't have a date during my high school and college days, I would join my rat pack and move from spot to spot until we found a "hot" machine. A "hot" machine was one that would give odds and features freely, at a minimum of quarters and nickels, and was easy to hit.

Necessarily for the successful existence of pinball operators, these were hard to find.

I sometimes remember playing 20-25 machines in the same night, and not straying more than about 12 blocks from Tulane's campus.

Names like Bahama Beach, Lido, Magic Ring, Safari, Big Wheel, Frisco City, Golden Gate, Surf Club, Roller Derby, and Zodiac bring back memories of OKs, Super OKs, two in blue scores 600 and red letter games we liked to hit.

Basically, the machines were money hungry – the more money you pumped into them, the better odds you got, and the better chance to win.

Often, it was advantageous to find a machine that leaned to one side or the other for certain types of shots, because the pinball tended to roll towards those preferable numbers. If it didn't lean, you could always make it lean by placing a bunch of washers under one of the legs. No one ever noticed.

And if the washers didn't work, you could use a brick or a book, if there was a big crowd around you. That really made it easy to win.

One thing about the bricks, they were a little bit tougher to carry around than the washers.

The pinball era is over, but with the word in headlines almost every day of the trial, it just kinda brought Spittin' Jerry back to mind. And a couple of his playing partners, like Fluff Shot Frankie and Luke the Cool.

An Alphabet Full of Blessings

December 23, 2007

A is for Audubon Park, azaleas, the Absinthe House, Antoine's, Arnaud's, Arredondo, Angelico, Aloysius, Algiers, Arabi, antebellum homes, architecture, ain't dere no more, Al "Carnival Time" Johnson, A.J., Ant'ny, Abita Beer and da Acme.

B is for the Big Easy, Bless You Boys, Buddy D, Bienville, Benson, Bayou St. John, beignets, bisque, Bananas Foster, brake tag stations, Barq's, Big Shot, Bob French, Bob Breck, Bucktown All-Stars, Bruno's, barbecue swimps, berled crabs, Benny Grunch, Bacchus, Bud Rip's, Brigtsen's, Mr. B's, Brother Martin, Barkus, Breakfast at Brennan's, Broussard's, Mr. Bingle, by ya momma 'n' dem, and Bagheads.

C is for Crescent City, the Cabildo, Canal and Claiborne, Chartres, Carondelet, Creoles, Cajuns, Clancy's, café au lait, the cornstalk fence, da Catlick Choich, Café Du Monde, Chris Paul, Cooter Brown's, C-Ray, Carnival balls, calliopes on steamboats, Chalmette, Commander's, cherce crawdads, City Park, Charity Hospital, Chopsley, Crystal hot sauce, Creole cream cheese, Camellia Grill, Court of Two Sisters, Crescent City Connection, Comus, and "Confederacy of Dunces."

D is for Deuce, Drew, dawlin', Dooky Chase, Deacon John, Dr. John's accent, dis 'n' dat, do-rags, Dillard Blue Devils, Downtown,

Donna's, Dixie Beer, De La Salle, Decadence, Delgado, Dan "Darn Scale" Milham, debutantes, dukes, Druids, duck season, dey all axed f'you, Deutsches Haus, D'Etat, Dilibonics, Dawlene, Dr. Nut, D.H. Holmeses and Dickie Brennan's.

E is for Emeril, ersters, erl, Endymion, Easton, Essence, and Euphrosine.

F is for French Quarter, French Market, Fats Domino, Fujita, da ferry, Faubourg Marigny, Fair Grounds, first you make a roux, Felix's, fishing camps, Foist Street, Fat Harry's, Frank "Natcherly N'Awlins" Davis, the Falstaff weather ball, Frankie Ford, Frostop and area code five-oh-four.

G is for gumbo, gris-gris, Gallier Hall, Gawlin & Angela, Galatoire's, Gentilly, Garden District, Green Wave, Gert Town, Gambit, grillades and grits, Gautreau's, go by ya gramma's house and Gretna.

H is for Hubig Pies, hawt, Hornets, a Helluva Hullaballoo, hurricanes, Harrah's, Hokie, Harry Connick Jr., Henry Butler, the Huey P., Holy Cross, the House of Shock, half shell, hogshead cheese, Hannan, Henderson's commentaries, Hap Glaudi, House of the Rising Sun, Hansen's Sno-Bliz, Hermes, House of Blues, ham sammiches and how ya'll are?

I is for Irma the Sweet Soul Queen, Iberville, da Irish Channel, Ignatius J. Riley, Indians, I done tol' you a hunnert times, Igor's and izzat so.

J is for Jazzfest, jazz and jazz funerals, Jesus Gawd, Junior, jambalaya, Jesuit, Jax Brewery, Jackson Square, Joe Krown, "Jingle jangle jingle, here comes Mr. Bingle," Jefferson and Jacques-Imo's.

K is for Kermit Ruffins, K-Paul's, K-Doe, krewes, kings, K&B, Krystal burgers, Krauss, K-Ville and another K we won't mention, because it doesn't exactly feel like a blessing yet.

L is for Liuzza's, Lucky Dogs, the Loyola Wolfpack, lagniappe, Landrieu, last call, Lee Circle, Lowerline, Lower Nint' Ward, Lucky Pierre's, Louis Prima, liver 'n' onions, Le Chat Noir, Langenstein's, Lenfant's, and Laffite's Blacksmith Shop,

M is for Mardi Gras, the Marsalises, the Mannings, the one and only Morgus, Mandina's, makin' groceries, Magazine, Mee-Maw,

Marie Laveau, muffulettas, mirlitons, mynez, the Meters, the Monteleone, Manuel's hot tamales, Mackel twins, McKenzie's, Moonwalk, Monkey Hill, Mr. Food, Maison Blanche, Mama D, Metry Cemetery, Markey's, Maspero's, Mandich's, Momus, Muses, Margaret "Get the axe" Orr, and mudda-in-laws.

N is for N'Awlins, or Noo Aw-yins or Noo AWL-uns or Noo Awlyens – anything but New Or-leenz — nutrias, Norman Robinson, neutral ground, Nint' Ward, nectar sodas, Newman, the Nevilles, Napoleon House waiters, and "No Left Turn" signs.

O is for only in New Orleans, "One call, that's all," Olympia Brass Band, Orpheus, O'Flaherty's, O'Henry's, Oliver "Who Shot the La-La" Morgan, ogle da goils, and oop-boop-a-doop.

P is for Pete Fountain, Pat O's, Parasol's, Professor Longhair, the Pontalba, pelicans, Palm Court Strut, Pascal's Manale barbecued shrimp, Preservation Hall, Popeyes, Port of Call, Pirates Alley, Proteus, da Pernt, Parkway po-boys, Privateers, and pistolettes.

Q is for queens, da Quarters, Quint Davis, and Quiche Lorraine.

R is for remoulade, Rex, Reggie, Rampart, Riverview, red beans and rice, Rock 'n' Bowl, rollin' on the river, Rib Room, Redfish Grill, red snapper, Ralph's on the Park's bordello mural, Rocky & Carlo's, R&O's, Rebirth Brass Band, the Red Lady, and Ramos gin fizz.

S is for Saints, Satchmo, St. Louis Cathedral, the Superdome, second line, streetcars, "Streetcar Named Desire," Sally Ann, Spud, St. Aug, Snug Harbor, Sugar Bowl, Snooks Eaglin, swimps, St. Jude, Sazerac, snowballs, stuffed eggplant, submarine races, sweet potatoes, Shinn, SUNO, Subdudes, Snell, da Saturn Bar, Schwegmann's, St. Joe's, sittin' on da stoop, squirrels, and say what?

T is for Tipitina's, Tulane, Treme, Tim Laughlin, Trombone Shorty, Tchoupitoulas, Topsy Chapman, Tabasco, Tennessee Williams, Tony Angello's, Thoth, Tujague's, trout amandine, trow me sumthin' mistuh, toikeys, turtle soup, Tuxedo Brass Band, Terrytown, terlets, tin ferl, tain't it the truth, and da Tenneco refinery.

U is for Ursulines, UNO, Ugly Dog Saloon, Upperline,

Uglesich's and memories of BBQ oysters.

V is for voodoo, Vaughan's, Venezia's, Vince Gibson, Vic 'n' Nat'ly, Virgets, Veterans, Vendome Place and Vince Vance & the Valiants.

W is for WWOZ, where y'at, Walmsley, Westwego, Wolfman Washington, Wild Tchoupitoulas, Whitney's clocks and who dat say dey gonna beat dem Saints?

X is for Xavier, and the "X" on your house.

Y is for Yats, Ye Olde College Inn, yams and ya know what I mean?

Z is for Zulu, zydeco, Zoo-To-Doo, Zimpel Street, Zurik, Zeke's, Zatarain's, Zion Churches and da zoo where dey all axed for you.

Reader Feedback:

Selecting five dozen subjects from more than 5,000 columns was no easy task. Did we leave your favorite one out? Send me a note as we start a second volume of readers' favorite columns. Your comments about this book are also welcomed. Send to: PrimeAngusLind@aol.com

— Thanks, Angus Lind